Together forever

The Gay Man's Guide to Lifelong Love

Martin Kantor, MD

SOURCEBOOKS CASABLANCA™
AN IMPRINT OF SOURCEBOOKS, INC.®
NAPERVILLE, ILLINOIS

Published by Sourcebooks, Inc.
P.O. Box 4410, Naperville, Illinois 60567-4410
(630) 961-3900
FAX: (630) 961-2168
www.sourcebooks.com

ISBN-13: 978-1-4022-0344-2
ISBN-10: 1-4022-0344-6

Library of Congress Cataloging-in-Publication Data

Kantor, Martin.
  Together forever : the gay man's guide to lifelong love / Martin Kantor.
     p. cm.
  ISBN-13: 978-1-4022-0344-2
  ISBN-10: 1-4022-0344-6
  1. Gay men--Psychology. 2. Gay male couples. 3. Interpersonal relations. 4. Love.
I. Title.

HQ76.K35 2005
155.3--dc22

                                                    2005025012

Printed and bound in the United States of America
VG 10 9 8 7 6 5 4 3 2

This book is dedicated to Michael.

Acknowledgments

I would like to thank my agent Barbara Levine, my endlessly patient and insightful editor Deb Werksman, and, no slight to either of them, most of all Michael, without whom this book would not have even been conceivable, let alone possible.

Contents

Introduction

Many gay men want to come out of the closet but they don't want to come out to an empty house. They want to put the gay scene behind them in favor of domesticity. They want to get a place, fix it up, and get a life. They want a rainbow flag over their door and a big presence in the supermarket and the social and political life of the town they live in. They want to join and gain respect from the community. Out is that lean and hungry look; in is an inner glow that proclaims "I am happy, I am content, I have found peace." They want altitude not attitude. In short, they want to get married.

Walk around some small towns with a large gay population, for example a community like the one we live in, Asbury Park, NJ, and you will soon see that a great transformation appears to be taking place that is changing gay life. Not only are rainbow flags flying outside of the houses of gays, in a gesture of solidarity they are also flying outside of the houses of straights. The bars are as much a place to greet as they are a place to meet. When the weather is warm you'll see little groups of people on the streets, a mixed group of gays, lesbians, and straights, animatedly talking with each other, the barriers down, no outcasts here. People are so friendly that after my partner Michael and I were introduced for the first time to a straight couple they went beyond merely saying "So nice to meet you" and, even though they didn't know us from Eve, took us on a tour of their recently renovated mansion in town. There are plenty of children around, but they don't always belong to straight couples. The parties are so mixed that a lesbian said to me recently about the straight host that "He knows more gay men than I do." Even singles are welcome everywhere because those already coupled are so comfortable with each other that they don't feel threatened by the competition. As for the political life, a third of the city council is gay, and at the swearing-in ceremony of a newly elected member his partner was at his side. The woman who just recently issued us a dog's license is the same one who just recently issued us a domestic partnership agreement, and not long before that was in the national news for issuing marriage licenses to gays and lesbians (that, unfortunately, didn't last long).

If this is a picture you want to be in as a married gay man, read on.

What is gay marriage? Gay marriage is almost the same thing as straight marriage, and not even the names have been changed. There are, of course, some basic differences, but central to both gay and straight marriage are the pinions of any great relationship: home, love, and stability, having a person you can count on to be there both when you are happy and when you are sad, and having someone with you beside a hearth that is always warm and welcoming in a place where you can hang together rather than separately. Friends come over for a quiet dinner on the weekends, and during the week you watch television and go to bed after the nightly news, knowing where your next romantic encounter is going to come from, and that you will be able to look forward to many repeat performances, which means you can practice until you can get it perfect.

Is this an idealized version of gay marriage? To an extent, yes, but it's not an impossible one. In fact, gay marriage is truly the answer to the many questions gay men have pondered through the ages. As a gay man, am I going to be happy forever, not just when I am younger? Am I going to be able to concentrate on my job or will I have to expend all my energy looking for sex? What happens to me should I get sick, and what, if anything, will I leave behind me when I die?

Of course, not all gay marriages are ideal. They range in quality from bitter to sweet, with a tendency to cluster at the extremes. The bitter you hear about all the time; you know, along the lines of dissatisfied house-husbands, with lots of cheating, an argument a day, and long, long, disappearances that make Anastasia look like an example of someone who is constantly underfoot. The depression and loneliness, anger and regret, rising expectations and dashed hopes are appalling, and the divorce rate is very, very high. Other gay marriages aren't as bad as that but they are compromises: working arrangements with lots of problems where even though the guys don't prosper they at least survive. Then there is the sweet; those blissful arrangements where married life is in effect that rare kind of buffet where you can both eat up and take home a doggy bag.

And the sweet is where I want you to be. If you aren't already married, maybe you want to read my book *My Guy*, about meeting Mr. Right. But if you are married, and your marriage leaves a bitter taste in your mouth, let's see what we can do about that. Let's see what can be done to make your marriage work, last, and be full of stability, love, trust, and, most of all, wonder, a thing that if it never ends, that will be too soon.

I want to make that happen for you like it happened for me. I have my gift, my own happy marriage of twenty-two years and counting, and I want you to have one just like it too. So, if you are having marital difficulties, either because of your or his personality problems or both, let's find ways to discover the happiness in what is already there so that you can keep joy, peace, and harmony in hand instead of letting it slip through your fingers.

A word about my style. If I make jokes, it's because I have found that sometimes the best way to convey truth is in jest. If I sometimes appear to be picking on you, it's because I know by experience that making your marriage work is often like going to boot camp. I know that because my psychiatric training has taught me that knowing yourself through and through, though it can be painful, is often the best way to solve your problems, my surgical training has taught me that in order to fix things right you have to first do a little nipping and tucking, and my obstetrical training has taught me that if you want to give birth to something really nice there is no way around the simple fact that before a new soul can emerge the old soul first has to go through a few nasty little birth pangs.

I don't have all the answers or the perfect solutions to all of your marital problems, and I can't tailor my suggestions to you personally, only to the average guy with an average kind of marital difficulty. As you will soon discover, monogamy is for me. But it isn't for everybody. Closeness is too threatening for some, too difficult for others, the wrong thing for still others, and anyway, not everybody can succeed even if they do all things right and all the right things. I can't promise that my methods will work for you. I hope they will but, after all, this is life and there are no guarantees. But I can promise you one thing. If they do work, and you resolve your troubles and put your marriage through the wash until it comes out clean, you won't think you died, only that you went to heaven.

A word about the terminology I use. As I said in *My Guy* there is no perfect label for two men in a committed relationship or the perfect name to give that committed relationship itself. Should one speak of lovers, significant others, boyfriends, partners, serious singles, spousal equivalents, or husbands? And are two men together in a partnership, a committed relationship, married, or what? I concluded: let me try to blur the distinction between gay and straight relationships by using the term "marriage" for both, and by speaking of "husbands," not "partners."

Is a domestic partnership as good an arrangement as a gay marriage? It's a fact that some gay men attach a great deal of significance to that one little word, "married." They feel that Shakespeare was wrong about that rose by any other name because if that were the case Francis Gumm wouldn't have had to change her name to Judy Garland. So they want to get "married," and to do so legally, just like straights. They like the status marriage confers on them as a couple. It makes them feel like a second-class citizen to be told that they cannot do something they want to do and that others can. They don't like being victimized by the homophobes of this world who fool themselves into thinking that they are hiding their bigotry and making it more acceptable by changing it over from "I hate queers" to "What's important is to maintain the sanctity of the time-honored tradition of marriage." Being practical-minded, they are seriously interested in more rights than the ones domestic partnerships can provide, so that they also want tax benefits, and such rights of inheritance as the ability to pass their social security on to their partners.

Therefore, it is crucial that real marriage be an option for those gay men who feel strongly that being officially married feels right. And if this is you, it should be available to you without your having to beg for it, or having to spend too many hours away from home trying to alter the political scene just to get something you should by rights already have.

But given the state of things in the real world right now, you, my reader, can, and maybe ought, to do some things to make changes. Personally, you have to set up internal firewalls so that it matters less what people think of and say about you. That way you can avoid having what the "big they" think affect your decision to live and love openly and to adopt children if you like. You can also consider getting involved in the political side of things, both because helping others strengthens you right now and because it makes the world safer for fairness, equality, and respect. So when, and if, you can, educate, help pass laws, write editorials and letters to the editor, give public workshops about gay marriage in general and what it means for you to be a married gay man in specific, and hit bigotry in the pocketbook by supporting businesses that are gay-friendly and boycotting those that aren't.

Of course, only do what you feel comfortable doing, and what suits your personality. As a matter of fact, this is a good rule that applies to all the suggestions I have for you throughout the book. Take from me what you find useful, and discard what doesn't work for you. But as you go along, keep an open mind, and be willing to try something a little different if it makes any sense at all to you. Be open to thinking inside a new box. I now offer you one for your kind, and I hope serious, consideration.

1

The Old Gay Scene or the New Gay Domesticity?

As a gay man, a wonderful lifelong relationship is within your grasp. A mutual, solid, and permanent spiritual and physical commitment awaits you. You can have that white picket fence surrounding that generic family of husband, husband, and two house pets. But you have to work for it, and on a number of fronts.

For one thing, you have to avoid falling into that all-too-common mindset where you become convinced that gay marriage is a joke with divorce the punch line, and that a committed monogamous relationship is for sissies, peasants, and Mr. and Mrs. Middle-America, with screwing around the gay norm, and staying around the gay exception. You have to avoid buying into the premise that gay marital vows are like the tax laws—everyone cheats, everyone breaks them, everyone winks, everyone turns the other cheek, and everyone wishes they could do the same thing.

For another thing, if you are already married in a committed monogamous relationship or if you are one of the lucky few who is actually legally married, you have to put the idea of getting a divorce completely out of your mind. Yes, if you are gay, divorce is easy, and even has a number of advantages. It can be a great way to get back at all those people (like me) who pushed you to get married when all you ever wanted out of life was just to have a little fun as a single guy. It can be a great way to punish a lover (and me) for—as you see it—controlling and criticizing you the same way your mother did. It can even be a romantic and dramatic magnificent personal tragedy, played out to operatic music in the minor key swelling in the background. But there is nothing magnificent, only tragic, about sitting there all by yourself at the neighborhood gay bar on Sunday morning drinking a bloody Mary with that limp celery stick with the fringe on top sticking wanly out of your glass—symbolizing, and all too well, your present life, and, even worse, previewing your entire future.

Yes, making your gay marriage work can be hard. Yes, marriage, gay or straight, isn't all great, and it isn't all fun. Which is why this book is not a feel-good book, you know, the "don't blame yourself if your marriage falls apart, not to worry, after all no one's perfect" type of thing, but a do-good book whose goal is not to make you feel better about your marital problems but to help you solve them. Take it from me. I know. I've been married, and I've been divorced, and I've gotten both on the same day, and let me tell you that when you have been happily married for twenty-two years and still going strong, as I am, and when you have had a lot of professional experience working with one or both partners of gay couples who only needed just a little bit of help to rescue their marriages from the edge, as I have, that the best idea of them all is to embrace this philosophy: "The worst day of a gay relationship is better than the best day of the Gay Singles Scene." There ought to be a bumper sticker!

So I have written a book with Attitude. It can be judgmental and contain some guiding principles that may at first glance seem unduly harsh. On the positive side, nonjudgmental books without the caveats and prohibitions you will find here allow you to keep your options open, foster self-realization, and encourage you to take charge of your own life. But on the negative side, in my professional experience as a psychiatrist, they don't offer those gay men who really need guidance the firm hand that just might rescue them from self-destructive floundering and a downhill spiral.

My book seriously pushes Donna Reed over *Sex in the City*, and the new gay domesticity over the old gay Scene. If you are tired of crocheting your wild oats and want to dance to a tune other than disco, if you want to stifle the inner gazelle in you so that you can at last leave the Tea Room and quit the Tea Dance for Tea Time with your very own appliquéd Tea Set in your very own special drawing room, read on and you'll see that I have some good ideas on exactly how to proceed.

To help motivate you, let me tell you about a bitchy critic of mine who felt that I was a killjoy, a tired old inhibited critical suppressive harpy out to keep the gay men of this world from having all the fun that goes along with and is the reason for being gay in the first place. Then one day his grandfather died, at which time he seems to have sobered up and changed his tune, at least for the moment. Now instead of his usual laurels to outlandishness and regularly spouted tributes to being single, wild, and promiscuous (believe it or not, one of his raves was actually about the wonders of attending a chubby convention made supremely fabulous— can you just imagine—by everyone's running around in their underwear), he seems to have turned serious, started reassessing his life, and begun wondering what was really meaningful in gay existence. As he put it, reviewing his own lifestyle, "I…work as little as possible, waste everything and spend most of my time worrying about the most trivial bullshit." Now he started calling having a wonderful wife, exceptional children, and extra-special grandchildren, the way his grandfather did, "cool stuff," and in contrast to that, in a transport of self-searching concern about "what I will leave behind," decided that his meager contribution to date to the world was "a stellar magazine collection, scribbles scrawled across the pages of a few publications and my uncanny knack for growing nose hair." Then he went on to say, "I'm not trying to belittle my existence. I'm just looking out at the homo-rizon and it scares me…I sure would love to live with the belief that, once I shove off this mortal coil, my life will mean something to someone other than myself."

So here comes my first and perhaps most important message. Don't let this happen to you. Plan right now to have a full, wonderful gay life meaningful not only to yourself but also to someone else, and do that by getting and staying married to your Mr. Right, your guy of your dreams. Then, when you approach those pearly gates and That Supreme Sissy in the Sky asks you what you have done to be proud of yourself when you were still on earth, you can swell up your chest with pride and say, "I gave him my all." And I just bet that now He, or She, thrilled to hear it, will welcome you into heaven, saying the words you should work a lifetime to hear, "Enter, for that was enough."

So let's discuss, "What is so great about gay marriage anyway?" It helps to first ask yourself, "What is so great about being single anyway?" To be absolutely honest, the answer is not nothing. There are some great things about being a single gay man. Yes, being single means being unfettered, like the dogs I sometimes see that obviously just escaped from behind their white picket fence, where they always had a cold lunch and a pat on the head waiting for them, now having all that fun, free as a birddog, sniffing everything in their path, oblivious to how their personal ball and chain, that collar around their neck with the dog tags, is the only thing keeping them from a trip to the pound, all expenses paid, you know, that other, real, cage, this one without that Judy Garland coffee table book, without the delightful line of gewgaws on the living room mantle, and without the shower curtain that to your infinite delight you made out of terrycloth towels sewn together in a beautiful mosaic that when the archeologists dig it up years from now will tell the world that a very special civilization really existed back in ancient Brooklyn. Yes, being single means being able to keep the bedroom at the temperature you like and never having to pick your clothes up off the floor. It means being able to keep the house as you want it and being able to sit surrounded by the things you love (inanimate department of course). And it means that you can put it everywhere you want it to go because, thankfully, your Designer forgot to install a one-way valve.

But think: is that really full compensation for the instability, aching loneliness, and various emotional diseases like depression and various physical diseases I don't have to elaborate on exactly that can be associated with being all by yourself, and for a lifetime?

Sure, gay marriage has its downsides. Of course, gay marriage isn't the perfect solution to all problems with gay life, and it does involve certain sacrifices. One downside is that being married makes you in some ways uncomfortably like your parents—a charter member of the square bourgeois middle-America establishment, the one that uninsightfully thinks that you, not they, are unnatural. And it does mean giving up some individuality, an act spiritually akin to physically fading into your flock wallpaper. You may have to put aside your dancing shoes and stop shimmying every night to the boogie-oogie-oogie. You have to at least occasionally close that zipper and reinsert that butt plug. There is some loss of freedom, having to live with a whole package that has some bad parts, and, depending on your personal arrangement, having to give up the undeniable highs of promiscuity for the undeniably same-old safe routine of monogamy. But there are downsides to everything. There are even downsides to wealth, good health, and personal/physical attractiveness. Wealth leaves you vulnerable to financial reverses; and good health and personal/physical attractiveness leave you open to having people use or stalk you. When it comes to gay marriage, you lose some freedom, you have to make some compromises, and you have to think of someone besides yourself. You take on some financial risk and you take on emotional risk too just by getting involved with and trusting another person.

Yes, I think that there are some meaningful drawbacks to being married, but in my opinion being single is always harder than being married, and a lot less fun. In my opinion, the negative aspects of a lasting long-term gay relationship pale beside the negative aspects of the single life. To me, the gay single life is the only jungle out there where everyone is at the bottom of the food chain.

So, instead of dwelling on the negative reality of being married to the point that you virtually create it, look at the positive aspects of having a wonderful long-term committed relationship and create that exactly. With those usual few exceptions that prove the rule, and excepting the usual downsides associated with anything less than perfect, which is most everything, marriage is right for many gay men, so that probably means you. Here is my checklist of the *good* things about having a permanent partner. Read and reread this list when your motivation to get and stay married flags, or if you are already married when you are tempted to stray. A permanent gay relationship:

- Is a sanctuary, your treehouse away from the rest of the world.
- Keeps you healthy and stabilizes you emotionally. You wake up every morning not having to panic wondering whose piece of bread your next crumb is going to fall from.
- Keeps you out of the bars living out that karaoke dream in song, and away from the streets looking for a hit.
- Keeps you better protected against getting physically ill from something transmissible.
- Keeps you from being deeply humiliated or seriously rejected by strangers. Now at least if you are humiliated or rejected it will be in the privacy of your own home, and from someone you know well

enough to have learned, at least a little, how to tolerate and, hopefully, even how to handle.

- Keeps you building a life beyond tightening your biceps in the gym and loosening your perineum in the baths.
- Spares you from answering ads for someone who likes candlelight and midnight walks on the beach, only to discover exactly why when the dawn breaks.
- Gives you lots to do every day and someone to do it with.
- Gives you that desirable entrée into the world of straight married people where as a single person you might not be so welcome. If you are gay it's a fact that many straights these days love married gay men and invite them over all the time. They include you in their functions because they feel it is okay with them if you are gay as long as you have a heterosexualized relationship, that is, as long as you aren't one of those stereotypical queers. Just recently even our president said something along the lines of "some of my best friends and even one of my political advisors is gay." Just imagine. Never mind that white picket fence. This sounds like an invitation to the White *House*.

But, alas, here you are. Every day is tense. The two of you, constantly on edge with each other, fighting, shrieking, demanding first your liberty then your Librium, and screwing and crying, screwing and crying—having an affairette, confessing or getting caught at it, making up, then getting guilty, then asking for forgiveness, then doing it all over again, all the while drinking heavily and even taking pills that your doctor didn't, because he wouldn't, or couldn't, prescribe. Chances are good that you think that this is happening because no gay marriage works, or that your gay marriage in specific is dysfunctional because the two of you are incompatible. But maybe there is another explanation. Maybe it's happening because you are confusing "My gay marriage doesn't work" with

"I don't work for my gay marriage," and "It's not right for me" with "For now, at least, I'm not right for it."

Working to make real changes in your marriage starts with day one, counting from the honeymoon. For good results you need strong resolve. There's no getting around it: making this particular omelet definitely involves busting your eggs. Marriage is not a pastime or a hobby, it's a full-time job. You may have to give up your skepticism and cynicism about those old-time virtues so often foolishly associated solely with successful long-term straight marriages—some very square things as it turns out, like a dollop of devotion to a cause, a glimmer of guilt, a mite of morality, a modicum of masochism, a smidgen of scrupulosity, and a wisp of the work-ethic. It involves motivation, which requires *sitzfleish*, that is, you have to have a big, soft, behind and be willing to sit on it until you get the job done. You have to take your marriage seriously, without treating it the same way you treat your back when you get into the shower—paying it no mind as if it will just take care of itself and remain pristine pure forever and all you have to do is pass your spinus divinus through the bathwater for it to magically come out clean.

Of course, motivation and effort aren't everything. It's not enough to want to do something and to work hard at doing it. You also have to know what you are doing so that you can do it right. You have to stop thinking only with your heart and your two other places (you know where they are). You have to be self-aware. You have to stand far enough apart from yourself to be able to do some serious soul-searching and some useful research into how you work so that you can view yourself dispassionately enough to enable you to identify *your* problems, not someone else's, in preparation for resolving them specifically, even though that means tolerating the considerable pain that is invariably associated with gaining knowledge and attaining self-awareness. You have to become sensitive to your partner's needs, which may mean developing more empathy, and you have to become more altruistic, which can entail making some sacrifices, starting with minor ones (like giving up style for substance to avoid putting the fate of your marriage after the fate and well being of your libretto collection) and going on to some really major ones (like putting his identity before yours). And you have to be willing to endure some setbacks and discomforts along the way. All this means you have to be a perfectionist of sorts: 100 percent firm about your desire, 100 percent clear about your goals, 100 percent honest when trying to understand yourself through and through, and 100 percent merciless when it comes to assessing your own contribution to any marital difficulties you may be having. You have to be a marriage partner full time, a guy who takes his commitment seriously and wholeheartedly. As I might say to you if I were Gertrude Stein, "Your commitment requires your commitment to your commitment."

You also have to avoid making serious mistakes that go beyond what is *unacceptable* to what is *unforgivable*—and there are two major ones in that category. These are hating him, either secretly or openly, and being unfaithful to him. When it comes to infidelity, a good general principle is that wandering eyes and wandering hands make for wandering off, so your task is to make his anatomy, and his anatomy alone, your destiny.

If you are seriously off base on any of these things, your job is to make any changes that might be necessary to avoid and correct marital difficulties. Start by checking off the items on the alerting psychological self-tests I offer you in chapters 5–13. This can help you determine if you or your partner occasionally go into one or more of the *danger zones* that I identify as potential sources of gay marital agita. But, please, don't let my checklists hurt or insult you. I am not trying to be critical of you or to excoriate you. I just want you to be honest about yourself, so that you can determine if any of the spiked heel shoes I lay out for you to try on happen to even approximately fit your pretty feet.

What do I mean by "going into a danger zone?" Through my work with gay men and in my day-to-day personal contacts with gay couples I have discovered that if there's one thing that threatens gay (and straight) marriages it's what I call "danger zoning." By danger zoning, or simply "zoning," I mean going into a kind of spell where you become difficult, often sufficiently so to create temporary or permanent havoc with your marriage. Some gay guys are always in a danger zone. Others just go into one or several zones suddenly but temporarily, then wake up to discover that they have made for relationship difficulties without even knowing what they were about.

Here are some examples of what I mean by danger zoning. Is hubby cheating on you? Maybe it's because he is a sexaholic. Or just maybe it's because you are currently in a "let's humiliate him" danger zone where you put him down instead of propping him up, and that's why he is out there desperately looking for someone, anyone, to admire him enough to make him feel like a big somebody, if only for the moment. Or maybe he is running around with neat guys because you are in your "slovenly" danger zone, having let your appearance go because "you already landed him, so why bother keeping it up?" If you are in this zone, you may not have to set limits on his behavior so much as you may have to set your hair. If he worries that he is getting older and becoming less attractive and less desirable to you, maybe you need to emerge from that "let's pick him to pieces" danger zone, stop complaining about his wrinkles, and start telling him that he is your beautiful Sharpei. If he is always doing the opposite of what you want him to do, maybe it's because you are barking marching orders when you should instead be whispering gentle suggestions. Is he constantly cleaning up around the house, putting everything away just after you lay it down? Maybe he is being too neat, or maybe you are being too sloppy. If you are in a too-jealous danger zone, you need to become more trusting, but if you are in a too-trusting danger zone you may need to become more jealous. I once had an alcoholic lover who went to AA where they told him that he, and he alone, was responsible for his drunkenness. But the truth was that I was behind the wheel driving him to drink. So the cure involved a thirteenth step, one they hardly mentioned: "sobriety" on my part as well as on his. Fortunately, I listened when he told me to lay off with the criticisms, and I responded by emerging from my "mean" danger zone, whereupon his drinking lessened, and, for a while anyway, that saved both our relationship and his life.

So if this is you, sober up, starting with remembering what so many gay men suddenly forget as soon as the marriage ceremony is over: that your husband is a human being who like anyone else responds to his environment. So, if you want a better response, emit a different stimulus. The question to ask yourself here is, "How can I stop making him crazy and start making him crazier about me?" and the answer to that question is: "If your guy is a tiger out of a cage, stop poking him and instead start taming him." First, determine where his sore points are, and second, apply your healing hands to those, exactly.

As I go on to explain more fully in chapter 3, there are two general ways to proceed. The first involves the use of generic remedies; that is, things that almost always work with almost everybody, preventing many or most marital troubles from occurring in the first place or rescuing a marriage already in difficulty. The central one of these involves harnessing the Power of Positivity, which, as I go on to elaborate in chapter 4, involves promoting healing using techniques of affirmation—tolerating his whims, gratifying his reasonable wishes, ignoring his less-than-serious zonal transports, and giving him lots of emotional support and positive feedback. I once had a patient who could do no better than complain that his lover put the keys down in the wrong place when the lover came home from work. My patient was actually getting ready to leave his guy because he refused to comply. He claimed that it was a matter of principle because if his partner really loved him he wouldn't do that, or anything at all, to upset him, even something small like refusing to hang up the keys on the hook dedicated to receive them. The relationship healed in large measure because my patient put principles aside, just picked up the keys, put them where he thought they belonged and wanted them to go, and then announced, in operatic tones, that "they have gone to a better place."

But if positivity with support and affirmation alone doesn't do it for you, you may have to try more specific remedies. That means learning all about the unfriendly danger zones I lay out for you, and discovering what gets you or him into and out of them. This, the best approach I know of for solving specific common problems associated with gay marriage such as Mr. Clean versus Dogzilla, is a great way to turn down the heat so that the both of you can happily stay in your kitchen. There are nine primary gay marriage danger zones, which are:

- Zone 1: Boredom and restlessness
- Zone 2: Sexual problems
- Zone 3: Anger
- Zone 4: Fear of closeness and commitment
- Zone 5: Self-absorption
- Zone 6: Being uptight
- Zone 7: Getting paranoid
- Zone 8: Excessive dependency
- Zone 9: Excessive competitiveness

But first, before you can know if you are in a specific danger zone, you have to be aware of the common myths currently in circulation about gay relationships. Myths are the misguided things you hear from your friends and read about in the many, not always completely reliable, books written about gay relationships. A typical widespread and very dangerous myth is the all-too-prevalent belief that the less dependent you are the better off your marriage will be, because all dependency is codependency and all codependency is sick. But in fact there is very little difference between closeness, commitment, intimacy, dependency, and codependency, so since you can't really tell them apart, just go ahead and be as dependent as you like, only making sure that your dependence isn't a danger zone for your marriage because in your particular case it works for one but not for both of you.

I have read lots of gay relationship books and they all tout at least a few of the myths I go on to describe. Some of them can be very harmful, damning a lot of potentially or actually great relationships to perdition. Because of all the myth-making out there I want you to be very selective about buying into the things you hear, which means disregarding the many misguided notions that have achieved widespread circulation and have captured the emotions and the intellect of some otherwise very sensible gay men. So think for yourself. Don't listen to the gurus who for reasons of their own, ranging from ignorance to envy, are trying to put a wedge between you and your guy. Instead view them, like the wedge they are trying to insert between you and your partner, as man's simplest tool. Don't let them create distance between your heart and your husband. Recognize that they have personal agendas that are not necessarily applicable to who you are and to what you as an individual want and need. Just dismiss them out of hand so that you can become the new, calmer and gentler, tamer married gay guy who fulfills the domestic vision that I hope you will come to embrace and share with me: you, him, the puppy, and the pussy, Saturday night, by the hearth, at long last out of the gay fire, and, into the new domesticity where I think you belong, back into the frying pan.

2
Myths and Facts

The story of gay marriage is rigged with false notions packaged as gospel truths that make a dangerous substitute for actual facts. Too often these false notions seep into an ongoing relationship to cause one or both partners to give up on their marriage prematurely, pack their bags, and head for divorce court before it is time to go. Some myths, like "everyone gay cheats on his husband even if they don't admit it," or "gay sex gets more and more tired and repetitive by the day, which is why one man is never quite enough," are mostly applicable to homosexual relationships. Other myths circulate about both gay and straight relationships, like "the best way to resolve relationship problems is to talk about them"; "it is perfectly okay to fight as long as you fight right and fair and according to time-tested rules of combat"; and "it is always a good idea to express the anger you have inside because anger when unexpressed goes underground, festers, and sooner or later surfaces in The Big Blowup."

What follows is a list of some of the most common myths about gay (and straight) relationships or marriages. If you want a happy long-lasting partnership, don't take them seriously, and don't live even a tiny corner of your life accordingly.

Myth: Long-term gay relationships don't work, so when it comes to gay marriage, pessimism is the operative word and breaking up the predictable outcome.

Fact: A relationship doesn't succeed or fail because of the sexual orientation of the partners. It succeeds or fails because the partners, whoever they are, make it a good or a bad relationship. Being gay is like being left-handed. Though you are different you are just a variant of normal. It may be a little harder for you to use the same tools that everyone else employs, but with a little extra effort and practice there is nothing that says you can't do the job. When the problems that surface in gay relationships seem unsolvable it is often just because you have let your relationship meet your negative expectations. If you think your relationship is going to fizzle you soon discover that, gay or straight, your pessimism is not merely a bleak evaluation of the past but also an alarmist self-fulfilling prophecy about the future.

The myth that gay marriage doesn't work is based partly on the statistical anomaly that results from only the bad news getting all the press. But you aren't a statistic, you are a person, and what's in the news may not reflect what's in your life. Anyway, even if the odds are against you, which they probably aren't, you can beat them, as long as you have a game plan tailored specifically to who the two of you actually are, not to some average abstraction of a gay man whose shoes don't fit your feet exactly, if at all.

Myth: Gay divorce is quick, easy, trouble-free, and without negative consequences. That's the nice thing about being gay—if things don't appear to be working out, you can just go right ahead and leave. Besides, you should do so now while you are still young enough to find someone better and bigger.

Fact: Many gay men who get a divorce now go on to regret it later. Their grief is intense and prolonged as they recognize too late that their first was their best partner, if only because he was at least the known devil. Therefore, feed yourself a lot of pleasure and save yourself a lot of pain by doing all you can to keep your current marriage intact. Make divorce court not a quick way out but the last stop on a train you refuse to board.

Myth: It's better to be single than to be stuck in a bad gay marriage.

Fact: I've known a lot of men in so-called bad gay marriages who still felt that they were better off when they were unhappily married than when they were single. In fact, the happiness of all the so-called happy singles I have ever met personally or treated professionally was at least partly due to their putting a good face on a bad thing, smiling in order to hold back their tears, going into denial about how unhappy they actually were in order to overlook how much they were actually missing.

Myth: To get along you have to agree on a lot of things.

Fact: It doesn't matter if you do or don't agree on most things. All you need is a few common interests to keep you going. My partner, Michael, doesn't much like classical music, so I listen to it on my personal stereo. I don't much like talk shows so he turns them on low when I am in the car. We both like disco (I am one of the older living true boogie aficionados through the ages) so that we listen to disco a lot when we are together.

Of course, you do have to basically agree on one thing: that your relationship is important and that if it is troubled you have to do something about it. You have to agree not to do what a patient of mine did when he screwed up a wood sculpture he was making in occupational therapy. He tried to throw it away, only I pulled it out of the wastepaper basket and told him to fix it, fix it right, and fix it now. He remembered that advice for a long time, and when he started having marital problems and thought that those too were beyond repair he applied what he had learned about the woodworking project to his marriage and also rescued that from the circular file.

Myth: A Great Relationship requires a Great Sex Life.

Fact: Aside from sex being only a part of marriage, that myth puts the cart before the horse. Because love is the fuse of a dynamite orgasm, it's

23

truer still that a great sex life requires a great relationship. Besides, after all, there is a middle ground between mighty multiple orgasms and the gay-guy version of lesbian bed death.

Myth: To be great, a marriage doesn't have to be perfect.

Fact: It doesn't *have* to be, but it *can* be, and you will both be better off if it is. So don't excuse your marriage's imperfections as par for the course "because all gay marriages are seriously troubled." Instead if something about your marriage is broken, be sure to go right ahead and fix it.

Myth: Even though your marriage has failed, you are not a failure.

Fact: You aren't a complete failure, but it's a bad start. You have, let's be honest, screwed up significantly. So let's face facts. Yes, you are still a worthy person, but there is every reason to learn from your mistakes, start doing things right, right now, and clean up your act before you drive him from your scene.

Myth: You can have a great relationship without it being a peaceful one.

Fact: Yes, you might be able to, but what would be the point? Peace, along with companionship, love, and sex, is one of the four main reasons to get and stay married in the first place. So don't listen to the gurus who tell you that it is okay to fight as long as you fight right and fair. Don't do what John did. From what he had heard, John thought that it was okay to fight as long as he didn't call his partner bad names and just stuck to the issues at hand. But John's partner Charles was an extremely sensitive guy who saw anything less than 100 percent positivity as 100 percent negativity, so as far as Charles was concerned, anything less than "I love you" became "I hate you." As a result Charles emerged from each one of their "fair fights" feeling lessened as a person and aching to find someone else who made him feel whole again.

Fights, no matter how skillfully fought, hurt and leave scars. The one and only rule that counts here is to control your anger. If you must get angry in the first place, keep your anger inside. Torquemada got his anger out, Mother Teresa kept her anger in. Now, if you had your choice, which one would you rather get to know? Don't worry that buried feelings necessarily build up to the point of exploding. Most things buried turn to dust. So here's another rule to go by: a stopped mouth is right twenty-four hours a day.

To anticipate my detailed discussion of anger in chapter 7, to avoid *feeling* angry in the first place keep trivial issues from assuming great importance. Also, get your priorities straight. Here is my list of priorities:

#1: Him.

Note that there's no #2.

See him as a whole person, not as a sum of his individual parts. If something he does makes you angry, okay, just blot it out with your memories of all the good things he did up until now and will likely be doing in the future.

If you find yourself feeling angry anyway, at least be certain to distinguish rational from irrational anger. Anger is *rational* when it's about something he did to make you really mad. Whenever possible, overlook that by being as tolerant and forgiving as you can possibly be and by not expecting him to be perfect in the first place. Anger is *irrational* when you are overreacting to something small or just reacting to nothing at all. It's irrational if he is late coming home because of an emergency at work and you get pissed off because you wanted to go shopping and here he is doing overtime because if he doesn't he will lose money or get fired, but you conveniently forget that, and think that he is deliberately making you mad when in fact you are just being too sensitive and overwrought. Remember the parable: There was once a little bird who feasted on horse manure until he was so stuffed he could hardly fly. He staggered to a pump handle, took a drink, and then flew away only to crash to the ground and die because he was so bloated from his opulent meal. That little bird had just learned one of the hardest lessons of life, and it's the one I want to teach you now: Never, never, fly off the handle when you are full of shit.

Now, if you feel angry, at least don't *get* angry. Put a cork in it, and simmer for a while until you calm down. But, if you can't keep from actually getting angry, at least channel your anger and get angry without blowing up. Yes, anger is a normal emotion, and we all get angry from time to time, but in my opinion, feelings of raw anger should never be expressed, for once they have come out they have created a black mark against a relationship, and that's one black mark that can fade but never disappear completely. So, if you just have to say something, simply say it on the fly and get it over with. A passing remark that smarts is better than a raging argument that starts. Better still, go to the gym, and exercise your anger away, or stay at home and punch a punching bag until you get all of your rage out of your system.

Myth: Gay romanticism and domesticity is an old and tacky concept, like Thousand Island salad dressing poured over a warm wedge of iceberg lettuce.

Fact: The best gay marriages are great romances in the old mayo and ketchup mix with a touch of pickle relish style. They are trashy and corny affairs that take place behind white picket fences with you hugging and kissing him as he goes off to work, and eyes fixedly looking into his, with more than just a hint of endless love welling up in your orbs for the photographer first, and for eternity next.

Myth: Gay sex with one man necessarily becomes less and less enthralling as time goes by.

Fact: Gay sex mostly loses its luster under three circumstances, and "as time goes by" isn't one of them. The first is when temporarily shattering circumstances preoccupy. That once happened to Ted and Mitch during a particularly difficult household move, but it all came back after they got settled and took their sex lives out of storage the same way they removed their possessions from boxes.

The second is when sex gets all wrapped up in guilt, which in some gay relationships can be a three-headed monster: your mother didn't want you to be gay, your neighbor in the suburbs doesn't want you to do "unspeakable" things in bed, and you yourself are trying to become a newly-minted saint—thinking that the worse your sex the better your chances of going to heaven.

The third is when you rely on bad advice from misguided gurus who tell you what to do about a flagging sex drive. There are many silly suggestions out there about how to do it better and enjoy it more, like taking up so-called new positions that you probably tried anyway on your own and found uncomfortable unless you happen to be a contortionist; pouring whipped cream all over him and licking it off without dropping the ball because you are giggling so hard; and, the worst, psyching yourself up sexually by flirting with other men, fantasizing a sexy porno star while you are doing it with your hubby, and in between events masturbating or even cheating as a kind of stretching exercise in preparation for the heavy lifting to come at home.

Do you really need books that tell you how to do it? After all, don't you pretty much already know what to do? I mean, really, now, aren't you already thinking exactly about what you would like to do all the time? Do you actually have to read about all the positions to take up one or more of them? Nope, you don't. You already on your own dreamed of falling heels over head in love, so what you are really looking for is permission to do what you always wanted to do, and it's very good practice to start getting the okay from within, just by giving yourself your very own go signal.

I have particularly serious objections to all the advice out there to look, flirt, masturbate with fantasies of other men, and cheat to your heart's content as a way to solidify your primary relationship. Those are artificial remedies that can work a little and temporarily, but they don't solve anything and they raise some serious problems of their own. The first problem is that if you give at the office you have less to give at home; it just makes sense that putting water in the soup makes it go around more but taste less. The second problem is that your partner is likely to be extraordinarily unfond of your extracurricular activities. Most partners take flirting as a sign of disinterest or as a warning that you are planning to leave them, and turning him off is not likely to inspire him to turn you on. Also, as for your masturbating away, wouldn't he have a field day now if he could read your mind about who and what you were thinking about? Actually, he doesn't really need to. He is your lover; he already knows. If he is at all the jealous type (isn't everybody?) he won't like your going at it with someone else in fantasy, and he may certainly resent it going down one drain when he really wants it to go up another.

Cheating, as I define it in chapter 6 is particularly bad for your relationship. Nothing that inherently immoral can ultimately enhance anything that inherently good. I would never cheat on Michael. Bad enough what it would do to him. It wouldn't make my heart grow fonder, it would break it.

I take up some solutions to sexual problems in chapter 6. To anticipate, while many people view loss of interest in sex with a long-term partner as the product of over-familiarity, I view it as the product of inhibition that keeps you both literally and figuratively from rising to the occasion, and therefore see the solution to problems with sexual inhibition not in aphrodisiacs like porn or vibrators but in chipping away at what is silting your sex life up—ranging from social approbation, which fortunately can be disregarded, to individual guilt, which fortunately can be reduced.

Myth: It's important to decide right now if the two of you are compatible and plan accordingly.

Fact: Incompatibility is not necessarily a fixed condition. So often what looks like incompatibility is in fact the product of an unfortunate dynamic interplay between two people, which, like any other interaction between people, is subject to change. So often an incompatible partner is like a ninety-eight-pound weakling, who with a little effort properly applied, can be molded into a beautiful muscular specimen. Flexibility, not compatibility, determines if you are right for each other. My own relationship illustrates this. My relationship with Michael was the first one of about twenty that worked and stuck. It did that partly because I finally got a clue as to how to behave, and partly because my guy knew how to make a compatible silk purse out of a once and former sow's rear. I am a very difficult person; like some gay men, easy to meet but hard to handle. But Michael knew how to treat me right to bring me around, turning me into another, better person, and he did that by following two main rules: overlook a lot, and neither piss on a dependent nor piss off a paranoid. As examples, he allowed me to cling all I wanted to, and he just stood there and listened to my rants without giving me a major argument. If he had pushed me away I would have recoiled. If he had given me an argument I would have gotten defensive. But when I saw that my rants were getting me nowhere I decided that it was a waste of time to carry on so, and just called that quits.

Besides, the rules about compatibility aren't very good in the first place. How are you supposed to know if it's "Opposites attract" or "Birds of a feather flock together"? And what exactly are the issues that are important enough to warrant concerns about compatibility? If you live more than ninety miles away from each other are you (like one guru suggests) incompatible? If he loves disco and you love classical music, are you incompatible? If he wants to adopt children, and you don't, are you incompatible? It doesn't depend on what you are now and want presently. It depends on what you are willing to become and accept eventually. Compatibility can be yours if you are willing to make your marriage a work in progress, where you learn and adjust as you go along, so that if column A doesn't go with column B you change what you put on your menu and how you serve it up. Raw fish doesn't agree with him? Steam his sushi. You and he are more malleable than you think and the experts suggest. You *can* change some people; and you can certainly *help* many others change. You can help make a dependent man more compatible with you by letting him depend on you more; an independent man more compatible with you by loosening his bonds; a suspicious man more compatible with you by becoming more trustworthy; and a stubborn man more compatible with you by avoiding confrontations. Often compatibility is little more than a matter of becoming comfortable with differences. You may never be able to see eye to eye on some things, like adoption, but you can almost always respect your partner's point of view, make compromises, and voila, live happily ever after as a couple. All you may need to do is to stop viewing your relationship as unworkable because you "don't get along" and think of your so-called incompatibility as a starting point for working out your interpersonal differences.

Larry was an under-reactor who never let anything upset him. He suppressed and denied how he felt about most things, saying "whatever," "it's what it is and we will just have to live with it," and "life happens." Craig, on the other hand, felt everything deeply and intensely, proof that you didn't actually have to be a princess to complain about that pea. Craig insisted that to be a good person you *must always* be in touch with your feelings, and that therefore Larry was not my kind of person because he was an airhead who couldn't say spit if he had a mouthful. Larry on the other hand condemned emoting as being something that was *only* for weaklings and so felt that Craig was not his kind of person because he was always ruining the scenery by turning over all the rocks. These two men were not terminally incompatible. They just needed to arrange themselves with each other as two people might arrange themselves in bed, testing out the different comfortable positions without overly disturbing their partner's rest until each discovered what exactly got the other comfortably through the night.

Myth: Being dependent means being codependent.

Fact: Healthy dependency gets a bad rap when it gets confused with unhealthy codependency. It's perfectly fine if you just can't live without him, but it's not so fine if you cling to him less because you love him and more because you hate him and feel guilty about it, and hang around him all the time to make sure that your hatred hasn't magically hurt him or in some way even killed him off.

Myth: It's a good idea to negotiate time and space to be alone.

Fact: Before you start this negotiation, ask yourself if you really want to be alone, or if you are just uncomfortable with being together. Ask yourself, what does your saying "I want to be alone" convey to him? Aren't you implying "You are getting on my nerves, so take off and let me breathe without having to worry about fogging up your lenses?" Now ask yourself, "Who wants to hear that?"

Myth: It's a good idea to pencil times for lovemaking into your schedule.

Fact: Doing that (as some gurus advise) straitjackets your emotions, which to be real, impressive, important, and loving have to be at least a little spontaneous. I think of all those people at the gym working out with their little charts, inscribing the last weight they did in stone, when all they have to do the next time is to get on the machine, try an approximate weight, see how that feels, and adjust the weight accordingly.

Concentrate your energy where it does the most good—away from your pencil, and onto his.

Myth: It's always a good idea to put your partner before your family.

Fact: It's possible, and sensible, to accommodate everybody here. Gay or straight, the natural course of events is to grow up in your family's home, and then, when you are just beginning to mature, to move out into a home of your own and continue the growing process there. Yes, when you first get married he will naturally be numero uno in all your thoughts. That is okay, but even then don't completely abandon your family. Coming out to them can be abrasive enough; leaving them for good can be devastating. Don't make your marriage an occasion to administer the coup de grace to them. Reassure them that they are not losing but gaining a son, and that as soon as you can you will be bringing them back into your life, although, of course, in a new and different, but not necessarily lesser, way.

Myth: Make many friends, and you will have an extended warm, supportive, loving family.

Fact: Friendships can be a wonderful thing. But the wrong friendships can endanger rather than support you and your marriage. So select your friends carefully, after reading chapter 14 on third parties from hell.

Myth: You have to love yourself before you can love him.

Fact: Self-love detracts from loving another. The truth is that to love him you have to love him, and you have to love him before you can even think of loving yourself.

Myth: Marriage keeps you from being you by interfering with your ability to maintain your identity as an individual.

Fact: Maintaining your identity at all costs is just another word for being selfishly concerned only with your philosophy of life, your self-image, your public image, and your ideals. Putting your identity first can mean putting your relationship last. In the beginning you may enjoy doing what you like to do whenever you want to do it, and being who you are no matter what, but later you will discover that doing what you want to do and being who you are isn't much fun if you don't have anyone to do and be it with. I have had many patients, ranging from straight women to gay men, who decided that marriage was stifling and that they just had to get out of theirs and be themselves. So, in their thirties, forties, fifties, and even after that, they started leaving home looking for self-fulfillment, dancing at the Crisco Disco, and doing that fatal needle exchange from knitting to hypodermic. Tragically, they gave up a stable long-term relationship for a series of short-term encounters, romantic on the surface but rotten to the core. Afterwards (many quit therapy because they felt that I was trying to keep them from flying) I heard that they were sorry and that they felt they should have stayed right where they were.

Don't let this happen to you. "We" is the most beautiful word in the gay lexicon. Repeat after me: being "us" is water. Being "me" is oil. You cannot "be me" and "be us" at the same time. You have to give up something to get something. You have to give up "marriage stifles the will-o-the-wisp in me" for "marriage brings out the best in me." As the Wall Street saying might go, bulls make money, bears make money, but pigs just squeal a lot in delight in the mistaken belief that they are on the way to hog heaven when they are really going to the slaughterhouse.

I go further into why marriage doesn't compromise your identity in chapter 8.

Myth: In relationships, honesty is invariably the best policy.

Fact: You can't go to jail for what you're thinking, unless you actually say it. For example, it is certainly unwise to tell your lover all your erotic dreams, and unwiser still to include in your little chitchat the names of any real people that are involved.

Myth: When something bothers you, communicate, talk, and discuss. That is the key to a lasting relationship, for unless you bring up what is bothering you tension builds and ultimately you explode.

Fact: That simple mechanical model compares the human mind, a bit anticlimactically, to a warm bottle of seltzer. In fact, communication is not the key to a lasting relationship. If communication is the key to anything at all it is to your single-room occupancy at the men's shelter. Discussing problems is not the royal road to solving them. It's the royal road to hell paved with bad intentions to say nothing of terrible ideas.

True, when faced with a relationship problem, most people first think to discuss it frankly, openly, and honestly. They say "Let's talk." They are sure that the discussion will end on a positive, happy note, the two of you in an emotional if not a physical embrace, and that all marital stress will be reduced or removed until marital nirvana looms.

But don't you believe it. It's just sugar-coated pop psychology that, as valid as it seems on the surface, can actually be very dangerous to the health of your relationship. For, in my book, discussions are not the way to nirvana, but to a nervous breakdown. Don't *speak* up; *shut* up, at least until you are absolutely certain of the difference between discussing, nagging, kvetching, and confronting. To illustrate my point that encounter sessions stressing open communication can be hurtful and insulting, here is the feedback from one such session held in a medical department with the goal of improving employee relations by getting it all out. One participant said it was a waste of time. Another was crying. A third up and quit her job.

Just for the moment, stop and consider the dark side of "Calling for That Discussion." Just "Calling for That Discussion" cannot help but by itself produce a negative response. And that's because your implication will be all too clear: something is wrong with our relationship and needs to be righted. Even if you are very clever about what you say later, what you have already said is too confrontational for comfort. The first words out of your mouth serve notice that you have weighed him in the balance and found him wanting. You have already said that there is something about him that you don't like. You have already put him down and told him that something about him is wrong for you. He already realizes that the discussion won't be about how wonderful he is. He certainly won't expect to hear, "I called you here today to tell you how much I love you and how much I appreciate your picking up after yourself and not leaving wet towels on the bed and letting me win arguments and not sitting in the car blowing the horn when I am late getting ready. That's it." He already knows: here comes Lizzie Borden with another hatchet. So he will feel cornered, and as if you are pressing both his alarm and off buttons simultaneously. Next he will get defensive and start working not on the problem that most interests you but on the problem that most interests him: how to at one and the same time protect his front and cover his rear.

Communicate all right, but only the good things. Don't tell him how you can't stand his snoring. Instead, wait until he doesn't snore one night then tell him how pleased you were about the quiet.

Dick tried to have a discussion with Val, his partner, only to discover how hard it is to distinguish "communicating with" from "crapping on." He thought he had it made because he had read and was closely following the advice in a self-help marriage manual on how to say bad things in a good way by putting mean things in an "I" context, not "Stop your snoring" but "I am an insomniac sensitive to noise"; not "Hang up your pants" but "I am the sort of person who gets upset unless there is a place for everything and everything is in its place"; not "You are such a slob, clean up after yourself," but "I really am nuts when it comes to liking a clean house and would so appreciate it if you didn't drop things on the carpet," then adding, "Perhaps I am a bit crazy in this regard, but try to humor me." He was proud of himself that instead of saying "Your vacuuming my office demagnetized all my computer diskettes" he would say, "I know it's foolish to brood that your vacuum demagnetized the only copy I have of my latest three volume romance novel, but that's the kind of thing I worry about anyway and just can't let happen." Dick thought he was using the cover of self-blame to avoid being coercive and demanding. But of course Val wasn't so insensitive that he couldn't translate, "I would like you to stop going to your room when you get home and closing the door and ignoring me for an hour; it makes me so upset" to "Quit it, bitch, or when you finally come out of hiding see if you can find *me*." Val, seeing through that little ploy, cut right through the sugarcoating and headed directly for the bitter core.

That's why I recommend something other than communicating. Instead of sounding off, consider why you might want to make noise in the first place. Certainly, before you say one word about being upset, make sure that you have a reason and a right to feel that way and are not just going nuts about something silly. When your lover snores, do you feel like killing him? Why aren't you happy that he is getting a good night's sleep, and why isn't that enough for you to be able to float peacefully off to sleep yourself? Is the answer that his snoring bothers you because you attach a sinister meaning to it? Do you become incensed at his snoring because you feel that the real reason he snores is because he is selfish and uncaring? Are you displacing your anger at your dog onto him, kicking him when you really mean to kick Buster? Are you dredging up the past, displacing your anger from a parent onto him, emptying your Louis Vuitton baggage from childhood all over your nice neat little life?

Make it a rule to only talk about what is bothering you when it *should* bother you. Having a conference when you are just being crazy about something minor or nonexistent isn't communicating; it's having a temper tantrum in public. So, determine if the problem is yours alone. Distinguish your rational complaints from irrational resentments, and, instead of discussing your irrational ideas, if you are the one who is without a queue, just wise up and get back into line.

Greg felt that he just had to discuss with Allan how much he hated it when Allan went off to a work-related convention. Greg felt that Allan would have said no to going if he had loved Greg more, and that if he didn't say no it was because he ached to get away from, more than he yearned to be home with, him. But Allan's boss had ordered him to go to the convention, and there was nothing Allan could have done to get out of it. As it turned out, Greg was in a chronic complaining zone because a few weeks earlier his boss had promoted someone else when Greg had expected to be the one promoted. Also, Greg, by nature a suspicious type, had pretty much become convinced that Allan was lying about the reason for going to the convention—as a cover for seeing an out of town somebody he was having on the side. Allan did finally manage to get away, only to have Greg call him several times a day to see how, read *what*, Allan was doing, and if Allan was out when Greg called, Greg would begin to think not that "the call isn't getting through" but that "he is getting it elsewhere." So Allan got peeved and, making a weak excuse for being delayed, came home a few days later than he would have otherwise. Therefore, Greg didn't have to have a discussion with Allan. He had to work not on his relationship but on his own personal problem. Greg had to have a little discussion with himself.

If you can't keep quiet, at least explain where you are coming from. Allan was unaware that Greg had been passed up for promotion, and might have been more understanding had he known what had happened and how badly Greg felt about it. Allan was also unaware of how possessive Greg was until Greg actually admitted to being jealous. After he realized it he was able to accept, integrate, and cope with Greg's jealousy. That's because like many gay men, Allan could accept a mystery as long as he understood its history.

Also, try not to call for a discussion the first time something happens. Let it go, hoping it won't happen again. Consider the possibility that by now he knows he displeased you, is already guilty about it, and is planning to stop it on his own. That way you can avoid having your complaints turn his guilt about something he did wrong into anger at something you did to wrong him.

Never, never, never schedule a later date for that discussion. By the time the discussion occurs he will be less ready for the straight talk than for the straitjacket. Every time someone tells me it's a good idea to postpone a discussion to a time when both of you are relaxed and ready to sit down and have a hard heart-to-heart look at your relationship, I tell them what my boss did to me once when he said, "There are problems with your job performance, and we need to have a little discussion about what to do about them. How about coming to my office soon so that we can have that talk? My next appointment is in two weeks." The next two weeks were like the hell of waiting for a biopsy report. If something needs discussing it's kindest to discuss it now. Besides, if you postpone the discussion it's likely that you will be saving and building things up only to hit him over the head with too much at once when it all comes tumbling out.

One alternative to having a discussion is to try finessing a problem. Uncomfortable with being alone? Don't complain that he stays too long at work. Instead get some mutually acceptable safe company, like a dog. If he puts wet towels on the bed, just get a water-resistant mattress pad and leave the towels there until he picks them up by himself. It's no big deal. They dry perfectly well in that position (although they might not be esthetically rectangular for the experience).

Another alternative is using psychology to avoid being punitive, judgmental, and coercive. Hook him into seeing things your way. Are you having agita about where to go for summer vacation? Perhaps instead of beating him over the head with how your ideas are better than his, you can talk up buying a house in Maine, getting him so excited about that that he will never want to go to Europe again. Perhaps if he is a decorating recidivist you can get him to go along with your idea of beauty by showing him a picture culled from *House Delicious* of a beautiful Bauhaus table with two lovely little sharp-angled salt and pepper shakers just waiting to be grasped by eager slimly elegant bejeweled hands. But your gentle coercive psychology must be entirely above-board. Don't leave out certain key facts or otherwise distort logic just to get him to change. Present your case honestly or he will see right through you, resent it, and dig in more deeply.

Or you can try to get him to identify with you and your stellar behavior. If he puts wet towels on the bed, remember that you have arms and can pick them up. Hopefully he will see that you don't like the towels there and be clued in enough to hang them up where you think they belong.

Or you can try positivity. This works with your dog when instead of hitting her when she does something wrong, you pat her on the head when she does something right. It'll work with many guys too.

Rolf's call for a discussion about his lover Phil's being personally messy and a slob around the house, as in, "You never clean the ring around the tub after you use it" produced a negative response in Phil because the implication was clear: something is wrong with our relationship and needs to be aired and fixed. Just by calling for the conference Rolf had already said his angry piece. Not surprisingly, then, as soon as the call for a discussion came in, Phil got defensive. He felt cornered. Anyway, he had been slowly becoming aware on his own of what was wrong and, already upset about having hurt Rolf's feelings, had planned to make it right without Rolf's having to say anything—that is, until Rolf said something, when Phil changed his mind, and started dragging his feet.

Come conference time, Rolf was careful about how he put things and made a real effort to present his thoughts nicely. But he was so angry that it was hard for him to present things in a civilized way. So Phil got the point that Rolf was furious. Rolf was turning up the heat to the extent that both of them started seriously sweating the small stuff.

I advised the two of them to take out their secret decoding rings and try to discover what was really going on between them by finding out what the real messages were that they were sending each other. As it turned out, the central problem was that Phil felt unloved because he felt that Rolf wasn't particularly demonstrative. Next, Phil got back at Rolf the best way he knew how: sensing how he could upset Rolf by not cleaning up after himself, he dirtied all he could just to punish Rolf for being such an ice-cube. I told Rolf that perhaps just saying "I love you" might be enough to call a halt to Phil's provocative behavior and the vicious cycles that it spawned. As it turned out, Phil was so starved for affection and love that Rolf only had to say "I love you" once before the situation turned around and improved as if spontaneously, and without the downside of a confrontation. "I love you" did more for the really important ring than all the best negotiations in the whole world.

So here is a checklist for you to complete before you have that discussion;
- Determine if what you are planning to discuss is *his* problem or *yours*. Are you sure you aren't the difficult person or the troublemaker here and blaming it on him, so that you don't need to start a discussion about what is happening, you just need to stop making it happen? Are you projecting—excusing yourself for something by accusing him of the same thing, turning "I want to cheat on you" into "I fear

that you are cheating on me" or "I am upset with you" into "Are you looking funny at me, as if I did something wrong?"

- Are you right to feel angry, or are you just being hypersensitive?
- Do you have rational complaints, or are your complaints really irrational resentments?
- Are you asking him to satisfy your legitimate needs or are you making excessive demands on him?
- Are you dredging up the past, displacing your anger from a parent onto him? Are you living in the past when you should be living in the present and looking to the future?
- Are you making him a scapegoat for something else going on in the present, say hitting up on him when you are angry with your boss?
- Would it help to just forget about a problem? I can remember a hundred big-deal issues in my life that I no longer even think about today. Then they seemed very important. Now I wonder what I was worrying about at the time.
- If there *is* a real problem with your relationship, is there a way to bypass it? Are you afraid of being alone? To some extent, we all are. But instead of taking it out on him for staying late at work, do what you have to do to realize your need for company. Get a job, or get a pet. My blood pressure dropped ten points after we got our cat. So did Michael's.

There are, however, times that you cannot avoid a discussion and you simply have to talk about what is troubling you. If that is the case, when you do have that discussion, have the best possible one that you can.

First try a simple exchange. Just calling what he is doing to his attention, saying the equivalent of, "Hey, what's up? This isn't the first time you have done that!" may be enough. Or just make your point on the fly, in twenty-five words or less, without making a big deal about things. Say your piece dispassionately so that you can put matters to rest quickly and efficiently.

If these things don't work, try using emotional filters to get your point across without being extra hurtful. A passive-aggressive emotional filter often works wonders by allowing you to express your anger covertly instead of openly. I go into passive-aggressiveness in greater detail in chapter 7. To anticipate what is in that chapter, when you complain, complain in the form of a question. Do not say, "You always lose something when you clean up my private space, so stop doing that," but instead ask, "It's okay for you to clean up my private space but when you do that can you please be careful to not move my papers around?" Say not "Gimme" but ask, "Is there some reason why I didn't get?" Demanding something is confrontational. Asking why you didn't get something is informational. Here's a game that sometimes works. If he makes demands on you to do something you don't want to do, instead of making him angry by saying "no" to the point that he becomes resentful and storms out on you, "yes" him to death, then drag your feet. Depending on who he is, he might hate that, or he just might appreciate how you didn't give him grief and, being full of appreciation today, start cooperating better with you tomorrow. Passive-aggression is not without its problems, and, of course, being passive-aggressive isn't as good as not being aggressive at all. But at least it's a gentle way to get angry, and gentleness is the hallmark of the good lover, and the balm and salve of a great relationship.

Get real about having a discussion. If he is cheating on you he is probably also lying to you about it, so why won't he lie to you again when you ask him to tell you the truth? In cases like this you might theoretically need a discussion, but speaking practically it might take more than a discussion to solve your problem. I go into what it might require in chapter 6 on resolving sexual problems.

Don't play the blame game. Don't claim that he is wrong and you are right. Refrain from critical verbal abuse and instead make this a session in which you negotiate and compromise. Focus strictly on present concerns, and don't dredge up the old tired critical stuff. Be specific, not general, about what bothers you and its possible consequences. If there are real problems try to come up with real solutions. For example, try, "When you were late yesterday, I worried about you" rather than "You never think of me, ever" so "Could you get a cell phone and call me up?" rather than, "Don't do that again." Also focus on realistic, not moral, issues. Is he cheating on you? It's not a sin, it's a bad idea. It has nothing to do with going to heaven and everything to do with going to divorce court.

3

Sailing the Seven "C's"

Are you having marital problems? Instead of breaking up and heading for divorce court, why not attempt to resolve them by giving my game plan a chance? I call this game plan "sailing the seven C's" because the name for each of the seven steps in the plan begins with the letter "C." My seven-step method is divided into two parts. The first part consists of three **generic** or "one-size-fits-all" approaches that can help prevent and resolve all, or almost all, gay (and straight) marital problems:

- Circumventing marital problems
- Coping
- Coddling

The second part consists of four **specific** approaches geared to precisely resolve the marital problems that result when one or both partners enter a specific danger zone, for example, when they feel bored and restless even though they are in a perfectly adequate relationship, or when they are so uptight that they make their partners nervous to the point of wanting to be cut loose:

- Catching zoning early
- Comprehending zoning
- Changing yourself
- Changing him

The three steps that are useful for preventing and remedying many different marital difficulties are:

Step 1: Circumventing marital problems

Circumventing involves not meeting marital problems head-on in an attempt to resolve them, but instead, taking tension-producers off the table. It means finessing problems instead of trying to iron them all out. It means sidestepping marital difficulties instead of trying to attack them directly. There are a number of ways to accomplish these things.

One good way to circumvent problems is to take positive healing unilateral action without prior consultation. Be there, be bold, be assertive, be definitive, but of course, be careful.

Problem: He comes home and goes to his room without so much as saying a word to you.

Solution: Knock loudly on the door, and sashay in, preferably scantily dressed.

Problem: His hygiene is poor.

Solution: Throw him in the shower and get in there with him. (That solves two problems, not just one.)

Problem: He is tightfisted even though you both have more than enough money.

Solution: Spend less, or make more, and if he is cheap, enjoy two living together as cheaply as one.

Problem: He is a workaholic.

Solution: Benefit from the financial fruits of his labors. If you hate being left home alone for long periods of time, get a second job so that you can be busy too when he is away and at the same time contribute some fruits of labor of your own to the household.

Problem: He is lazy.

Solution: Fill in for him and do the jobs he doesn't do himself.

Problem: He is on a different schedule from you, for example, he likes to sleep late when you like to get up early.

Solution: Find something to do while he is in bed, like some useful work around the house.

A second way to circumvent problems is to set a good example for him. People often act like the people they are with. Make what you do a portrait of how you would like him to act with you. If he is always late, be on time yourself, then compliment yourself within his hearing range for being so prompt. Your hope is that he will learn by osmosis, and become just as sweet as you are.

A third way to circumvent problems is to focus attention away from the problem itself and onto its solution. Just recently our ladder was stolen from our terrace. Michael, who is far less paranoid than I am, said he thought that the builders next door took it by mistake. I said that I thought that the crooks in the neighborhood took it on purpose. What is really important here is securing not agreement but the new stepladder.

Reverse psychology is a fourth good way to circumvent problems. If he won't get up on time Saturday morning to do the household chores, instead of nagging him with lots of pleas and whines, tell him it's okay for him to sleep as long as he likes. Your hope is to undercut any stubbornness fed by his pleasure in getting a rise out of you. Or, play the game of "you are right" where you agree with what he says not because he is correct (which he may or may not be), or just to shut him up, or to give him carte blanche, but to keep him from having fun at your expense as he enjoys pushing your buttons so that he can turn you on then sit back and watch you squirm.

Step 2: Coping

Coping with what cannot be changed starts with redefining love as the ability to get used to almost everything. It involves just accepting him as he is and learning to live with it. If your guy turns you off by looking like a slob, instead of criticizing him, decide to accept his appearance as it is, and maybe even offer to buy him some new clothes or give him a gift certificate to the new spa. Of course it also helps to be a laid-back relaxed type so that you can zone out when he zones in. When I asked one gay man who was successfully married the secret of his success, he answered, "I learned how to put up with a lot." As he in essence put it as we were terminating after a successful year of therapy, "Every road has its potholes. I stopped thinking each time I hit one that my undercarriage was now completely shot. I realized that I would never get where I wanted to go if I got hysterical thinking that every little bump in the road had ruined my entire trip."

Phony dramatics, with a dollop of humorous irony that turns the sublime into the ridiculous, are often a good, if somewhat insincere, way to cope with relationship problems. You get things off your chest and at the same time make your point without belaboring it, all in an acceptable, roundabout fashion. Weep crocodile tears and act tragically wounded, saying, "Boy, you really know how to hurt a guy," or "Boy, you really know how to leave me hanging." Tearfully remind him of the extent of your self-sacrifice, while at the same time pointing out that while human sacrifice appeases the Gods, it tends to seriously displease the victims.

Another form of coping involves simply agreeing to disagree. If you don't see eye to eye on something, don't fight about it, just accept that with most things there are two rights and two wrongs. When Michael is more positive about people than I am, I don't feel that I have to bring him around to my way of thinking, haranguing him until he views human nature the pessimistic way I see it. Instead I accept that two people can have different takes on the same reality, meaning that a pessimist who always anticipates the worst and takes precautions just in case can live comfortably side-by-side with an optimist who doesn't worry about things that are probably never going to happen anyway. Instead of doing follow-ups to decide who has the real word, we just lay back and let life, and our differences, wash over us. It's partly that differences of opinion are rarely a big deal. It's also that if we disagree that just makes us *both* birds of a feather that flock together *and* opposites who attract.

It helps you to cope if you remember that most zoning is neither permanent nor all-inclusive, for partners go in and out of zones quickly and when in them still retain plenty of surrounding softening matrix, what we refer to when we say things like, "I still love him, even though from time to time he can be a real bitch."

Step 3: Coddling

Coddling may be the single most important method of them all for making your, or any, marriage work. It's the opposite of after saying "I do" forgetting that what he does is a response to what you just did. Coddling involves accommodating, which is a form of catering to your guy by giving him what he wants, and taking care to not deprive him of what he likes and needs. It also involves reassuring and supporting him in order to calm his fears. If your guy is excessively suspicious of you, instead of complaining that he doesn't trust you, tell him not to fret then act in a way that reassures him that he doesn't have anything to worry about. If your guy is in the "uptight" zone, so that he starts worrying that he left the stove on as soon as you drive ten miles from home on the start of your long-awaited two-week vacation, don't slam into him for being a silly alarmist but instead humor him by turning around and driving back to check the flame. You will certainly save your marriage, and you may save your house too. Once when we were fifty miles away from home Michael began to wonder if he had left the basement window open. So we turned around and drove back, and guess what. There it was, the ladder we had just used sticking out of the basement, right through the window we had left wide open. Is your husband insatiable when it comes to needing love? Don't tell him to stop hanging on your tits. Instead provide him with relationship TNT: Two Nifty Tits to hang on. Does he feel so lonely that he is constantly nudging you by putting you on speed dial and calling you up all day long? Before he speed dials you, take the initiative, and dial him speedier.

Coddling is primarily based on the principles of positivity and affirmation I outline in chapter 4. Here's that positivity principle in a nutshell: you catch more flies with honey than you do with horseshit.

The next four steps involve specific relationship remedies geared to resolving defined marital problems that are the product of the nine common types of zoning I outlined in my introduction and will elaborate on further in chapters 5–13.

Step 4: Catching zoning early

A good start to making repairs to your marriage involves spotting zoning and its effects before vicious cycling takes over and causes irreversible rifts. As I started telling you about in my first chapter, gay men (like anyone else) go into a temporary or semi-permanent emotional state from time to time or live in a permanent emotional zone resulting in interpersonal behavioral patterns that have a fixed, repetitive, compulsive quality. These zones can come across as grafted on the trunk of one's personality ("He gets pissed off from time to time but otherwise he is a pretty nice guy, overall"), or as an integral part of the personality itself ("He's just not the faithful type"). In the first instance it's pretty clear that your guy is currently possessed, while in the second instance it's often very hard to tell what is "him" from what is "the devil inside of him." The individual so possessed often suspects that he is not quite himself, or that the self that he *is* is not the self that he *wants to be*. But he feels helpless to do anything to change. These zones are generally associated with negative implications, but of course there are positive aspects to them too. For example, being uptight is annoying but it can also lead to enhanced creativity and functionality.

Because all of us have a distinctive personality, there is no one right and no one wrong way to be. Just because one or both of you are zoning your way into specific marital problems does not mean that the two of you are incompatible either. It doesn't necessarily signal the presence of irreconcilable differences. It may not even mean that your marriage is in trouble. It simply might mean that you are dealing with two shticks rubbing together and rubbing each other the wrong way. For even if both of you are not on the same page, you can still be in the same book.

Step 5: Comprehending zoning

Dealing with the marital conflicts that result from excessive and persistent zoning involves understanding the zoning process through and through. In turn that involves decoding the messages that zoners are deliberately or inadvertently attempting to send. For example, when two men live together, often the utility bill comes in one name only. You think that he would want it to be yours, so you graciously volunteer to be the one who gets billed, only to have your partner go into the competitive zone, bridle, and complain that you are acting like he doesn't count and trying to make him invisible. If you truly understand that he is a competitive guy who hates your having something that he doesn't have, even if it is only the telephone bill, you won't get mad and scream, "I thought I was doing you a favor." You will instead do something counterintuitive, and graciously offer to put the telephone bill, and maybe all the other bills, in his name.

Step 6: Changing yourself

Changing yourself, a great idea when most of the zoning is yours, involves growing, or growing up, within your relationship so that your relationship can in turn grow up and around the new you.

Billy, a patient of mine, got a divorce because he never learned how to stay married to his husband Steve. Billy liked Steve, only he didn't much like his toupee. It turned him off. He said he looked great without it, so why was he wearing it in the first place? I asked him, "Why don't you tell him to get rid of the rug?" He said he didn't like to tell people what to do. He actually told me that he would rather get a divorce than have to go through with letting Steve know that he looked ridiculous. He explained his reluctance to speak up as follows: "If he were a really good guy he would know not to wear something so stupid-looking without my having to tell him." So after four years of marriage Billy invited Steve down to meet him on one of the docks in town and told him, "It's all over between us." To the end Billy insisted that his valor was the much better part of discretion. He said he needed a new marriage. But what he really needed was not a new marriage but a new and better attitude about his old one. Billy didn't need to change his partner. Billy needed to change his personality.

Sandy could have improved his relationship with Matthew a lot by becoming just a little bit more understanding and a lot less critical and devaluing. It was true that Matthew was an uptight guy who got very nervous about everything. But it was also true that Sandy was too stubborn, inflexible, and rigid for his own good, and for the good of their relationship. One day Sandy, who had to be out of town for the day, asked

Matthew to take their adopted child, Selena, to the orthodontist to have her braces fixed. He also asked him to wait with her in the waiting room for the three hours it would take for the work to be done. Matthew, balking because he had a full schedule of work that day, was low on leave time, and feared being fired from a job he really needed, suggested that they have a mutual friend take Selena in and wait there with her until she got finished. But Sandy wanted the personal touch, and nagged and nagged Matthew until he finally agreed to go and wait with her himself. Afterwards Sandy, checking up on Matthew, speaking to the kid within Matthew's earshot, asked her if her father was a "bad boy" who shirked his responsibility or a "good boy" who took her in as promised and waited there with her the whole time.

Not only was Sandy distrusting Matthew, he was also infantilizing and demeaning him. So Matthew began to feel emasculated, and decided that a little proof that it was still intact down there would be just the ticket. Matthew, looking for someone else to help him feel whole again, had a series of affairettes. Matthew hadn't become a sexaholic. Matthew had become a henpecked husband who finally decided to stop scratching the ground in abject humiliation and to start looking for emotional support outside the coop. The first line of defense was not for the two of them to consult with a marriage counselor. For starters the solution was as simple as having Sandy back off and be a bit more flexible and a lot more understanding.

If you sincerely want to change, start by asking him to critique you so that you know exactly what to do to clean up your act. Ask him if he has any complaints about you and listen to what he has to say without becoming defensive and grousing that he is being punitive and judgmental. Take some responsibility for your marital problems. If you must play the blame game, at least try to play the solitaire version.

Step 7: Changing him

Changing him, or, better still, helping him change, is a good idea when he is the main one zoning and you aren't a major contributor to the process. Contrary to popular belief, and to what you have probably heard and read, at least some types of partners can change, and you can help the process along if you know how to do it right. Of course, it's not possible to change every partner. Stubborn partners are particularly resistant to change. But in contrast flexible or dependent partners are generally willing to do anything to win and hold on to their partner's affection.

Helping him change doesn't mean nagging him to "get a clue." It doesn't mean controlling, punishing, or squelching him. It does mean helping him grow by providing him with the proper growth medium. Start by not ignoring, minimizing, or making fun of his problems. Never tell him he is silly to think and feel the way he does. Take his anxieties seriously. Ask him to take any criticism you might have of him as a constructive heads-up bumpy-road-ahead alert meant not to make him feel sheepish and defective, or to threaten him, or to unleash self-criticism, but to encourage self-observation. Tell him you are not being a knuckle-rapping parent lodging complaints about him or condemning him for being bad. Remind him, over and over again, that you are just trying to help him do better.

You can often help him change by improving the way you treat him, using a combination of the generic measures I outline in steps one through three (positivity in particular) and the specific methods I outline in chapters 5–13 geared to actual marital difficulties (for example, being 105 percent honest with a guy who is suspicious). Always keep in mind that more than likely his difficult zoning is the product of his feeling miserable inside, so that a good start in the direction of helping him change is first to find out all about the pain in his heart, and then to do everything that you can to ease it.

For example, you might reassure a worrisome guy, "Even if you did leave the coffee pot on back at the house, nothing is going to happen for the hour or so that you are out shopping," and, even better, get him the kind of coffee pot that shuts itself off automatically. You might pull back to avoid arguing with a stubborn guy, the kind of person who can't help but respond to anything you ask of him as if you are trying to control him, leading him to dig in and refuse to budge. You might offer a suspicious and even a mite paranoid partner complete accountability, for example, taking care not to be constantly primping to the point that you give him the impression that you are trying to look good for some little thing you have on the side. Give an independent man some breathing room but not so much space that he feels you are letting him rattle around and get into trouble. If he is independent because he doesn't trust you, become more trustworthy. If he wants to be dependent on you but fears you might feel overwhelmed, offer to let him cling, and never distance yourself too much from him in any way, especially by threatening to leave him.

Try helping him change by osmosis. If he is a pessimist, encourage him to be an optimist by being more positive about things yourself. If he is inhibited, encourage him to be more spontaneous by being less uptight yourself. If he is a big worrier, help him relax by not taking everything so seriously yourself.

This said, it's important to realize that some partner zoning responds poorly or not at all to certain remedies, which you therefore have to avoid. While it may be a great idea and very productive to discuss problems with a dependent partner who hangs on your every word, discussing problems with a hypersensitive suspicious partner might just upset him even more because to him it means that you are not for, but against, him. Too often discussions spin wheels with men who are in the uptight obsessional zone, merely covering the same ground over and over again without breaking into any new and useful territory. Making lists and keeping journals is a great idea for most people, but once I suggested that an obsessive-compulsive guy do that. He followed my recommendations, only he followed them in spades, and to this day he is still trying to make page one perfect.

This book is all about staying out of danger zones or getting out of them once in them. We'll focus on generic positivity as a good general way to handle almost any relationship problem. We'll also focus on spotting and handling the nine most common danger zones that trouble gay marriage, like boredom and restlessness, or suspiciousness and blaming. I include checklists to help get you started thinking about yourself, your partner, and your marriage. Check off the items, and follow the instructions to see if what follows applies to you or your partner, meaning that one or both of you might profitably look further into the matter. These checklists are not scientific psychological tests designed to uncover big psychological problems and make precise diagnoses. Rather they portray little slices of life that characterize the main danger zones that can lead to gay marital angst. Be honest when you check off the items in these lists. This is not a popularity contest, it's a self-evaluation experience, a heads-up overview to see if you might need to have a long, close, hard look at certain aspects of yourself and your relationship with the ultimate goal of uncovering sources of tension between two basically compatible guys and making those changes, which can be small ones, that can in turn make for big improvements. For example, if you are a hothead constantly shifting over into the anger zone, you don't have to turn into an inert gourd, let alone into a pumpkin, to significantly improve your relationship with your partner. All you may need to do is to channel your anger into a less interpersonally disruptive mode of expression.

Some of my checklists are short and some are long, depending on how simple or complex, that is, readily identifiable or obscure, the zone in question happens to be. Not surprisingly in a book that emphasizes problem resolution, my checklists tend to focus on negative over positive characteristics. But that doesn't mean that the zones I describe don't also have positive value, and in fact there is a thin line between good things like intense love and problematic things like excessive dependency. Also, since we all are prone to one or more danger zones, a positive response to many or even most of the elements in a list or lists doesn't mean that you are abnormal. It just means that you have hit upon a fertile field for further exploration, and that just means that together you and I have uncovered a great place to jump in and get started turning your marriage around.

4

Coddling: Positivity and Affirmation

Some gay men believe that just the idea of being positive and affirmative to their partner is terminally corny and uncool. But in my experience the power of positivity and affirmation is so great and works such magic that it can by itself turn a difficult relationship into one that is passionate, perfect, and permanent. I have found that positivity and affirmation are among the best ways to overcome the three strikes that many gay relationships start off with: no legal constraints to hold you together through difficult times; no children to sacrifice your individual happiness for; and no social sanctions to discourage you from breaking up for the flimsiest of reasons.

There were many occasions when I saw the marvelous effects of positivity and affirmation help married gay men overcome their differences and other apparently insurmountable obstacles and stay together anyway. A particularly notable example involved Gene and Matt. When they first came to me they had so completely started off on the wrong foot that the beginning of the end was in sight. It all began at the wedding ceremony when Gene said "I do" to Matt—only to get Matt's name wrong and call him Mike—the name of his last lover. Matt stayed angry with Gene from that day on. After a few months he went at Gene's throat over stupid things like, "You always clean up and put my stuff away then I can't find it when I need it." Then he started threatening to walk out on Gene over nothing at all.

Here are some of the main components of the principle of positivity I recommended to these guys and can almost without reservation also recommend to you if your marriage is presently in difficulty or if you see trouble coming and want to stay out of it.

Stop all your fighting

Many gurus reassure you that it's okay to fight as long as you fight fair and fight right. They define fighting fair and right as sticking to the subject, avoiding playing the blame game, and discussing only practical issues while simultaneously avoiding moralizing. But never mind fighting right. It's a bad idea to fight at all. That's because you can't do something wrong the right way. It's a fact: any fight, fair or not, brutalizes your guy and your relationship. Yes, you can get away with one or a few fights on occasion, but sooner or later you can no longer wipe the slate clean and go back to square one. You have done some permanent damage to your relationship, and afterwards while things may seem okay they will never be exactly the same. So, if you are fighting a lot, do what you can do to tame your, and his, fighting spirit. As an example that anticipates my discussion of anger zones in chapter 7, if your guy is a lion on the loose demanding to be dominant, try being submissive—offering him your tender underbelly, anticipating that he will accept that as your willingness to surrender, and will now calm down, as if by magic.

Overlook a lot for the sake of your relationship

Because all relationships have flaws, the two little words that can make all the difference between a relationship that works and one that doesn't are: "So what?" Say them and you won't care so much about little things that don't really matter. Say them and your temptation to snap at crap will be over. Say them and you will be more likely to look at the big picture and recognize that what's important today usually doesn't count for much tomorrow. Make it easy to say them by saying to yourself, "It's not worth aggravating myself over that," and "It's just the way he is and I can adjust, accept, accommodate, and get over it." Make molehills out of mountains as you willingly overlook and forget the niggling details of who is doing what to whom, who did what first, who is the victim and who the victimizer, and who is to blame for this or that. Instead of noticing the minor things that do, and even should, bother you, let them pass. It won't be the end of your life, and it just might be the beginning of your new and better relationship.

Jack and Frank had an argument about whether Frank should consider an upcoming convention a fun or a working vacation. Jack wanted Frank to say he was on a working vacation because, secretly incensed that Frank was leaving him for a few days, it made him feel better to think he was doing it for work, not for pleasure. But Frank kept insisting that he needed the rest and that he was going to have fun even though he also had to work. Sadly, they just went on and on trying to iron this little wrinkle out, when that well-timed "So what" would have stopped this silliness dead in its tracks.

Every time Hal comes home and walks in the door, he hits Morey with a criticism like, "If you leave the screen door open like that the bugs will get in," or "It's hot in here; why do you have the heat turned up so high?" or "It smells in here; have you been cooking asparagus?" Morey doesn't say anything. Instead he sits on his anger until it goes away, which takes just about a minute. He tells himself, "So what," and that "looking on the positive side, we can, after all, always live happily ever after together in the small hot cottage with the little bugs and the big smell of delicious asparagus cooking."

Kyle is always late to appointments. Stan, his old lover, constantly flared because of that and eventually decided that it was reason enough to leave him, for as Stan put it, "If he really loved me he would make sure to be on time, all the time." Frances, Kyle's new lover, just doesn't care. He doesn't get angry then make excuses for his anger like, "Everyone in a similar situation would feel hurt and insulted." Instead he tells himself that his relationship as a whole is more important than this particular part of it, and that it's worth losing this little skirmish about time to win the much bigger war about love.

Try using a little psychology

Try **positive conditioning (positive feedback).** Look for the positive aspects of what he says and does and respond only to those. Compliment him when you feel he has done something right, but don't say anything at all when you feel he has done something wrong. When you call him up does he put you on hold unnecessarily? Hold your water, act like nothing happened, then wait until he stays on the line with you without interruption and say how much you appreciate that. Don't tell him you don't like it when he doesn't shave. Instead each time he does shave, say "You look so good that way, so sexy. Hint, hint, hint."

Try **reverse psychology**. If he is acting too independent for your tastes, say, "Go out, I want you to enjoy yourself, and have a good time, I need to stay home and finish my Afghan anyway." Though you are probably at home sweating, your hands too shaky to crochet, he doesn't know that. More than likely he is not having the good time out he could have had if he thought that his being gone bothered you at least a little. So he might just come home sooner to see if you are still there anxiously waiting for him. Now you can put down those boring needles, welcome him back, say how happy you are that he returned early, and gleefully anticipate that the next time he won't be in such a rush to leave.

Is he eating too much or not the right foods? Try nagging him to stop and see where that gets you. Or try saying in a loving way that you want him to be around forever, so you hope he won't die before his time and leave you a grieving widow with the condo and all his fortune, with you perfectly situated to purchase a nice shiny new thinny-thin boyfriend with very, very low cholesterol.

Reverse psychology works particularly well with people who are contrary enough to most want what they feel they cannot have or are about to lose. It is useful to get a partner: to stay home when he wants to go somewhere without you ("go, if you would like, I have plenty to keep me busy here"); to stop attacking you verbally and physically ("I can see why you are angry with me and I don't mind because I deserve it"); to clean up around the house and to keep his personal hygiene up ("In my book, cleanliness is next to nothing"); and to be less remote when you would like him to get closer ("You don't have to fawn and slobber all over me all the time, you know, I can take care of myself.") It's not at all useful when the cure is worse than the disease ("Let's spend it all until we have nothing left," or "We don't have to have sex, I don't care that much about sex one way or the other"). Also, not all partners react favorably to reverse psychology. Spero was one of those people who are chronically late, about an hour exactly each time, and nothing worked to get him to come on time and to stop calling to say he was just leaving when he should have been just arriving. So Mike had only two choices: ignore his lateness, or stop seeing him entirely. Also, when reverse psychology backfires, which it can, watch out because you will be getting what you say you wish for when that is exactly the opposite of what you really want.

Try **leading by example**. Bring him around by osmosis by becoming a good role model for him to follow. Show him how you would like him to behave toward you by behaving exactly that way toward him. If you want him to clean up around the house, clean the house up yourself. Call if you are going to be late, hoping he will pay you back in kind. Don't expect immediate results from this method. Sometimes it takes months or years for him to get the point and even longer for him to return the favor.

Try being **passive-aggressive**. If there is a choice, sometimes passive-aggression is at least gentler than raw aggression. For example, instead of saying "no" to a request of his right off, just stall. Telling him "No; get lost," can be very provocative. Silence or a non-committal smile can produce winners all around (although the method isn't perfect). I discuss passive-aggression and its pros and (mainly) cons more in chapter 7.

Change your environment for the better

Better your life together by making your surroundings more livable. Don't have that fight about what to watch on television. Just get two television sets and each of you watch exactly what you like.

Accommodate

It's a fact that healthy accommodating is a great way to resolve the differences and conflicts of will that crop on a regular basis in all relationships, and maybe most of all in relationships between two men.

Accommodating avoids two generally imperfect alternatives: dominance and negotiated compromise. Dominance builds resentment. Negotiated compromise leaves two people with one thing neither of them fully wants. He wants to go to South America, you want to go to Maine, so you go to Bermuda instead because it is part way between where he and you really want to be, leaving both of you incompletely satisfied. In accommodation you might take turns. You go to South America one year and Maine the next year, leaving each of you completely satisfied, if only half the time.

Accommodation consists of two major components: empathy and altruism.

Empathy involves guessing where he is coming from without his having to spell it out for you. You put yourself in his place to see exactly what he is all about. You are alert not only to how something affects you but also to how the same thing might be affecting him. For example, Ricky instead of getting annoyed that Franz was late coming home from work one night, reminded himself that Franz's being stuck at work was as much a problem for Franz as it was an inconvenience for Ricky. You intuitively understand why he feels the way he does and why he does things his way even though it's not your way. For example, Josh complained that Bruce didn't fold the towels after taking a bath. Instead of making a pretty neat rectangular hanging masterpiece, he hung them open on the towel rack, each with its end messily jutting out over the sides of the rod. It took Josh some time to finally understand where Bruce was coming from: fold the towels and they never get dry, and become moldy and unpleasant to use the next time. You willingly respect differences instead of selfishly complaining "my way or the runway." In Josh's case, this meant realizing that "neat as I like it" was a very narrow, very "I" view of how things should be, and one that overlooked other viable and even possibly preferable takes on the matter.

Altruism starts with being cooperative. A good beginning is not making the "I do" of your wedding day the only and the last time you say "yes" to anything. It involves prioritizing your relationship, putting it first without getting sidetracked by More Important Major Issues, not putting your marital promise after some big-deal philosophical premise.

It involves not standing your ground just to make an intrinsically correct but adversarial point, being practical over being idealistic to avoid sacrificing your relationship on the altar of some purely theoretical greater moral or spiritual good, ranging from "monogamy is not part of the gay identity" to the self-homophobic "Man should have kids, so I'll go straight, drop Louis, and marry Louise."

It involves giving your guy what he wants even if it's not exactly what's right for you and even though it deprives you of something you want and need. For example, Michael and I recently discussed moving from a nice quiet little house by the river in the woods to an apartment in a small-sized city by the railroad tracks in an urban renewal zone (read, the slums). I started bitching like crazy about leaving the pastoral scene behind for the noise, chaos, and danger of the new place. Then Michael confessed that he really never liked the house. It was too much work to keep up and too expensive to run, and our new apartment-to-be was much more convenient and practical. So I changed my attitude completely and decided if not to love then at least to accept the change—simply to make him happy.

Clearly altruism involves your being more concerned for him than for yourself. Even if it inconveniences you, if you sense that he is upset when he leaves for work you call him up just to say hello and find out how he is feeling. It also involves a degree of self-sacrifice—for example, because you have to take time out from your busy work schedule so that you can make that call. Certainly don't demand that you both go to that mid-week concert you simply have to hear if he has to go to bed at 9:30 p.m. just to be able to get enough sleep so that he can get up early to be at work on time the next day. Don't stop him from decorating his way if that is what he likes to do. Let things into the house that are not really your taste. You can live better with a piece of furniture you hate than without a person you love. Or, suppose it's Christmastime, and you are faced with another bad trip to your in-laws. Go anyway if it means a lot to him. You will get through it, and he just might adore you for making the attempt.

Neil hated the gym he and Fran used to attend. As he put it, "The people there aren't very nice and some of them are truly weird. Can you believe that one guy actually went from machine to machine with an emery board and a bottle of nail polish doing his manicure between sets? Also, they scream at each other and talk so loudly on their cell phones that it makes the tower of Babel seem like a rest break at the morgue. They also hog machines, using them as a personal throne from which to hold court, as they loudly as well as haughtily and mightily congratulate themselves for being wonderful while condemning everyone else around them for not matching up." But because Fran liked the place, and because it was the only gym in the area that he would agree to attend, Neil decided to wall off the annoyances as best he could and keep on going for Fran's sake.

When exactly should you give in and accommodate? You should give in and accommodate when you are just going through a phase so that in a few months you will no longer want what you want today. As the old saying might go, there is nothing worse than getting what you wish for the day after you stopped wanting it. Give in when whatever happens will not be so bad anyway. Ask yourself this: "Just how serious and important is this thing that I am getting all bent out of shape about?" Identify when disputes are, like decorating disagreements, about insignificant things. Recognize that in the infinite scheme of things such things don't really matter so much, and that even if they do there are ways to make them matter less after the fact. Besides, not only is it not that hard to come around to liking your man's preferences, allowing yourself to be led in small ways today sets the stage for a newly cooperative venture tomorrow.

Give in too when his being out of line is the exception rather than the rule, and as payback for his having just accommodated a little to you. Also give in when it's for the good purpose of doing something truly great for your relationship, such as not hurting his feelings, or sparing him ongoing displeasure.

Certainly give in when his needs are far greater than yours, as when he has emotional problems that at least for now he cannot help. Be extra-sensitive to what makes him anxious, depressed, or paranoid; speak to his needs even when they are excessive or childish; and don't ask him to get over something he cannot master. Never criticize your guy for being a certain way. Instead try to see where he is coming from and steer him in a better direction. If you are wavering here it might steady your resolve to keep in mind that his being difficult may not be directed to you personally but instead may be the product of something he is going through inwardly, and in spite of himself. So, instead of condemning him for being bad, actively look for an emotional explanation of what you at first might be tempted to dismiss as his "misbehavior" so that you can help him do better. High yield areas here are sexual jealousy, paranoia about fairness, and conflicts over dependency.

As examples, Sean understands how dependent his lover Roy is and leaves a note for him when he goes out on the terrace just so that Roy doesn't wake up and find himself alone for fifteen terrible seconds. Jack does a reality check for his partner Ted by gently refuting Ted's unrealistic jealousy. Instead of telling Ted that he is being oversensitive and imagining things, he tells him that he doesn't need to be so afraid. For example, when Ted thinks Jack's eyes and mind are wandering, Jack doesn't say, "Stop being so jealous." Instead he reassures him of how much he loves him and that he would never think of doing anything to hurt or deceive him, while at the same time he makes himself accountable and available 24/7/52/365/50+.

Marlon refused to go to James's favorite restaurant because Marlon believed that while the waiter always asked James if he wanted another cup of coffee, the waiter never asked Marlon if he wanted another drink. James was tempted to globalize and tell Marlon, "You never do anything I want you to do." Then James realized that Marlon was very sensitive about being ignored, and just decided to find another restaurant.

I know that I am being difficult and neurotic when I start worrying about whether Michael has arrived safely when driving to work, especially when I worry about it even before he has had enough time to get there. I know that I am just too easily panicked and foolishly irrational because I leave no margin for his getting coffee, bringing in his cleaning, or being unavoidably delayed in traffic. So I try to stop worrying; but I cannot. Matters improve when instead of complaining about my behavior Michael humors me. He knows that I have a problem I cannot easily overcome, so he helps me cope with it. He gets a cell phone and calls me up if there is a delay—and sometimes even just to give me a progress report. I also have a phobia of driving, which I will never get over. Instead of insisting I get better so that he doesn't have to be my chauffeur, he just drives me around everywhere we go.

In his turn, Michael doesn't particularly like flying. He and I flew to San Francisco then he spent the next seven days worrying about getting home. We had a beautiful home on Long Island, in the woods, but Michael became fearful at night that an animal would come out of the woods and attack him. What did we do? Send Michael off for emergency psychotherapy or for drug treatment? No, we stopped traveling and sold the house. While I miss the trips a little I can forgo them, and while I loved the house a lot, it is only Michael who loves me back. Michael was neurotic about the trips and the house and I wasn't, but I don't think that the "abnormal" one has to change. I think just the opposite: that the "normal" one has to change because the "abnormal" one cannot help himself.

It is especially important to be willing to bend a little and accept those quirks and differences that are culturally-determined. For example, I have that uptight New York tendency to overreact to everything, while Michael, coming as he does from a Southern background where people at least seem to remain relaxed until there is a real reason to get upset, is more laid-back, sometimes to the point of not anticipating difficulties that could have been avoided. He needs to reassure me when I worry too much, and I need to worry for both of us when he doesn't want to be bothered.

When you have questions about who should accommodate, keep certain likely defaults in mind. For many people not putting wet towels on the bed is a better idea than soaking the mattress, and "don't worry too much" a better idea than "worry constantly." I was counseling Jimmy and Seth. Jimmy was an uptight worrier and Seth was more relaxed and even fatalistic about most things. Jimmy thought it was good to worry because that way all the bases were covered, but Seth thought that it was bad to worry as if every game needed a rain date. Jimmy preferred to anticipate tomorrow while Seth thought it was a good idea not to think about tomorrow in order to be able to have a more pleasant today. So on a regular basis Jimmy would scream "You never take precautions in case" and Seth would scream the equivalent of, "You are always ruining our bridge party with your constant worrying that the cops are about to look under the bridge." I had Jimmy divide the pages of a notebook into two columns and on the left make a list of what he worried about during the last month and on the right a companion list of how things actually turned out. Now Jimmy began to see that almost nothing he worried about ever happened, and that the few bad things that did happen were those he didn't even think to worry about. As a bonus, when Jimmy began to worry less, Seth became more willing to evaluate each situation on its merits and to become truly concerned when real trouble loomed.

Sometimes it's not immediately obvious who should accommodate. An example involves the Romantic Parable of the Ficus Tree. I love ficus trees and Michael hates them. I, of course, am right. After all, they are beautiful plants that arch gracefully over the furniture giving all they touch a *House Gorgeous* look, so that by getting one and placing it properly in a smart corner of our room I have clearly done something so meaningfully artistic that it is worthy of its own website flagged number one on Yahoo. Of course, all I have really done is quite routine: the equivalent of completing a picture in a child's coloring book, painting by the numbers, or connecting the dots to make a line drawing. Michael is also right. Ficus trees are a cliché, rarely seen now because they are a nuisance. They drop their leaves and always manage to get scale, which is the equivalent of plant leprosy; or they get spider mites, giving a new, deeper meaning to the concept "website." So what to do? Michael and I had a short, not heated, discussion about this. We decided to compromise, that is, we both decided to accommodate to an extent to each other. I could keep a slip I rooted from a ficus cutting a neighbor had put out in the garbage if I put it in my office where he wouldn't see it, and lived like a man with the consequences if it got sick or died, which included having to pick up the leaves as they fell, dabbing the insects one by with rubbing alcohol if it got scale, throwing out the carcass afterwards should failure occur in spite of all (and that without sticking the twig in my eye if I bent over to see if it were still alive), and agreeing to forgo grief-counseling and to put up with its demise without over-bitching about having a brown thumb, or how that if God really loved me he would have kept my tiny little baby alive.

Self-sacrifice, an extreme form of accommodation, is an especially

71

useful technique for dealing with transient relationship emergencies. If used carefully and selectively it has very little downside. It stops fights and arguments cold letting both of you get your bearings, at least momentarily, which may be enough. Some people would call those who too willingly self-sacrifice "masochists." I feel that at least under some circumstances one man's masochism is another man's getting along famously.

Here's what accommodation isn't. It isn't about having, and losing, a power struggle. It doesn't involve permitting yourself to be severely abused just for the sake of your relationship. It doesn't involve playing games you cannot win, like accommodating to sadists, if only because that can have a paradoxical effect, with your being too willing to put up with too much encouraging a hate-filled guy to take advantage of you. It isn't giving in when the principle of the thing is less important than the thing itself. You can't be physically hit, not only on principle, but also because it hurts, or kills. It is not being a patsy, a wishy-washy person, a sap, a pushover, a nonentity, or a dominated weakling playing the foil to a partner who wants to be impossibly strong and dominant, and it doesn't mean you are failing to protect and maintain your macho image with friends and family, if only because most people don't really care about you and your relationship and who is the top dog as much as you think they do. It doesn't mean failing to protect your identity, especially that sort of identity that rises and falls based on such trivial issues as who picks the menu for the next dinner party, and it doesn't involve appeasing and surrendering to a parent substitute all over again. Also, it's not completely and foolishly unselfish, containing as it does the seeds of plenty in it for you, however much the rewards come later—tomorrow, not today. As for the latter, for accommodators, being a pushover today, if that is what you are, should be part of your grand plan to selfishly assure your happiness eternally, as you give in today on the less important things, things that require no real sacrifice on your part, so that the important things will be there for you tomorrow, making you in effect not a masochist but a shrewd manipulator, someone who knows that to reel in a fish if you yank it, it will get off the hook, but if you give it play and let it run now you can better run it in later.

Try taking the following quick quiz to see if you are or are not a true accommodator. Choose the one answer that comes closest to what you would do.

Your lover leaves his clothes all over the place and you like a neat house. You handle the situation by:

1. Saying, "You are such a slob, cut it out."
2. Saying, like you read in the last gay guru book, "We must have a discussion right now about this significant matter" or, if you are busy now, "We must have that discussion later in the week, so let's set the date now for later." (Overlook his sulking as he wonders what in hell you are going to talk about when the discussion finally happens.)
3. Discussing things, like the gurus suggest, by putting them from an "I" perspective rather than from a "you" perspective, apologetically blaming not him but yourself, as in, "I like to have things straight; perhaps I am a bit crazy in this respect." (That "I" trick ought to fool him good into thinking that "I" aren't a bitch.)
4. Speaking your mind right now because, having heard that even lovely aromatic lilies when buried start to fester and stink, you feel it's important to say what you mean, and to clear the air, even if that means clearing the room.
5. Getting quiet and starting to sulk. He knows something is wrong, but at least you didn't criticize him or actually have a fight.
6. Leaving the clothes there until he puts them away or they rot,

whichever comes first.

7. Grinning and putting the clothes away yourself, right out of Disney singing "Whistle While You Work" as you toil away at your happy little task.

Only one of these approaches makes you a true accommodator. Which is it? (# 7, Walt.)

In conclusion, accommodators:

- Are long-term planners: short-term losers of battles but long-term winners in relationships.
- Within relationships, don't select, but settle.
- Overlook a lot for the sake of their relationship.
- Accept less than perfect when it comes to his flaws and are instead forbearing, willing to ignore or accept his imperfections, just as they want him to ignore or accept theirs.
- Remember that the difference between a relationship that works and one that doesn't is the willingness to tolerate the forest for his tree.
- Willingly make the adjustments and exchanges necessary to keep their man happy.
- Willingly are empathic altruistic generous individuals even to a fault, the big one in their relationship, in the hope, and often in the justified expectation, that the relationship will expand to fit their size.
- Role play to first discover and then second speak to their guy's sensitivities and avoid poking his sore spots.
- Willingly bring their lover around by giving him what he wants even though it is not what they want, knowing how good a return on their investment that is. They volunteer to get screwed one way this time so that they can assure themselves of getting screwed another way, another time, and for a lifetime. He isn't into the Scene? So what. Just change the scenery.

When Michael and I have our decorating disagreement about ficus trees, I talk to the ficus tree, and I say, always remembering what it was like to be alone before I got married, "I am sorry, Brenda (all my plants, except the venus flytrap, have women's names), but he is right to hate you for being a ficus tree. Even though I love you and think that you are the ultimate accessory, if you don't fit into his grand scheme of things, you will certainly fit into the consignment shop."

Treat him as an equal

Never subjugate him. Don't make him your maid. Bend down and pick up after yourself and, if he is the sloppy one, after him. The goal is to have a neat place and a neat relationship, not one or the other. Don't divide the chores along the lines of "I do the clean stuff, like pay the bills, and you do the dirty work, like clean the bathrooms." Don't ever live in an apartment where you and only you hold the lease, or in a house where you own the whole thing and he chips in to help pay expenses without building equity.

Don't compare him to others

He is who he is, not an inferior version of someone else.

Say something positive to him at least once a day

Every day say at least one thing nice to or about him. For example, tell him that you are his and his alone. We were invited to a big gay bash for the Oscars. I asked Michael if he was disappointed that I said I wasn't interested in that particular party. He replied, "I am home with my baby, what more do I want?" What more do I want?

Say something nice not only in words but also by facial expressions, and by such actions as touching. Go ahead, be corny. Corn is a basic foodstuff, so dish it out liberally. Build him up with strokes. I remember having an old lover who was cheating on me. I deserved it because I was such a mean, critical, SOB. I could have rescued the relationship if only I had stopped and said just one nice thing to or about him. But instead I became more and more vituperative the more he cheated, further lowering his self-esteem, giving him a new and better reason to cheat on me. It might have all stopped if I just once told him that I thought he was a great guy and that I loved him. Almost certainly he would have started loving me back, and then he might have thought twice about continuing to cheat on me.

If you can't get loving words out of your mouth, ask yourself why. Is it because, fearing the love inside of you, you drive him away so that you don't have to love him so much? If this is you, tell yourself you have nothing to fear but fear itself, and an extremely messy divorce. (I discuss fear of loving at length in chapter 8.)

Be complimentary to him whenever you can, and never criticize him for anything at all

There are three different nos. There is a "no" that is a critical attack, there is a "no" that is a command, and there is a "no" that is a corrective. The first is "No, you idiot." The second is "No, don't do that." The third is "No, that's not the way to do things, this is much better." The last "no" is okay; the first two "nos" are no-nos.

Never, never, say anything extremely negative about him, either to his face or behind his back to a third party, either vocally or by sending nonverbal messages. If you don't have something nice to say, say nothing at all. This is partly, hopefully, because you have nothing bad to say. It's also partly because if you badmouth him to other people and have it get back he will know what you really think of him, and that will forever diminish his respect for you and hurt him badly as he discovers that he is coming up short in your eyes. Never do what a famous movie star's husband did: he told the media that his wife was difficult to live with. Maybe, just possibly, if she was, it was because he provoked her by saying mean things like that about her, and to the whole world yet.

If you feel he has done something wrong, first make sure he didn't do what he did because he misunderstood or misheard you, or because you never explained yourself to him in the first place. Now, if you are still certain that he did something wrong, don't bark at him. Instead of criticizing, attacking, and humiliating him for what he hasn't yet learned, teach him what he needs to know. Educate him without being harshly judgmental or punitive. You would be surprised how easy it can be to say or do something that humiliates your guy. Once I said to two married guys, "I am writing a book about keeping your relationship hot" and they both rushed over to talk to me, as if it were an emergency. I wonder what each of them thought afterwards about what the other one had in mind. Your being neurotic is no excuse for mistreating him either. He is a real person, not someone you conjure up out of your past or from bad feelings about other people, like the boss, displaced onto him. Just because you have baggage from long ago doesn't mean that you should treat him like some old baggage rack.

Try to put a good spin on everything, or at least almost everything, that he says and does. Review your negative impressions of him and ask yourself if there is a simple, more positive explanation for what at first appears to be negative behavior on his part. Is he late coming home? Do not think or say, "You selfish uncaring miserable bastard," but instead think, or say, "You must be upset about not being able to arrive on time, the traffic must have been terrible." Be charitable. If he does something wrong then says, "Boy, am I dumb," respond, "No you are not, you just made a mistake, and anyone can do that." If he says, "Wasn't it stupid of me to lose the car keys and now we cannot get home," say, "Everyone loses things." Once when I spilled my coffee Michael didn't scream "You idiot." What he said was, "I do that too from time to time."

If he thinks that he did something to upset you, tell him that you don't mind. Say, "I might prefer things to be otherwise, but I have come to accept that that's just the way you are." If he says, "I just dropped my pills on the floor and the dog ate them and now it's a big vet bill," say, "Life happens." In short, give him the benefit of the doubt, absolution when he feels guilty, and reassurance and compliments when he feels self-critical. If you say nice things about him that make him feel good about himself, the next thing you know, he will become just as good to you as you just said he was.

Don't trivialize his complaints about other people. Take these complaints seriously. Never say, "It's not important what they think, so you shouldn't give a damn." Always say, "That's terrible." Take his side whenever possible. That's because if you aren't for him he will feel you are against him. Do everything you can do to avoid making him feel that you are defending them instead of him, taking up their cause instead of his. Your lover complains, "Your mother is a bitch." Do not respond with, "Only when you upset her." When he complains that he feels rejected because his mother hasn't called for three months, and asks "What do you make of that?" don't reply as if it is okay for his mother to ignore him; don't say "All mothers go through stages like this occasionally." If he complains, "All your family talks about is their boring granddaughter" don't reply as if its being widespread makes it all okay; don't say "Most people with kids do that." Don't do what Sam did. Once Jud complained that a colleague was taking too much sick leave, leaving Jud with all his work, and his lover Sam responded, "Perhaps he is really sick." Jud shot back, "Only on

Fridays?" to which Sam responded, "Yes, because of all the tension during the week." It would have been much better if Sam had said, "You must be very upset. That guy sounds like a loser." Taking his side works because it helps enhance his self-esteem. It uplifts him. Here it's more important to be spiritually correct than to get all the details right.

In your turn, be open to constructive criticism coming from him. You might not like to hear your lover's complaints about such things as the style of clothes you wear, but you should determine if his criticism is valid, and, if it is, hear him out and do what you have to do to change along suggested lines. Once I tried to wear a dress shirt with shorts. Michael said no way, and by now you should be able to figure out what I said in response. Was it:

1. I am an ivy-leaguer who always wears button-downs on top no matter what goes on down below.
2. I wear what I want and do what I want to do, so either put up with it or get out of my life.
3. I set the styles for fashion; they follow me.
4. Thanks, you just saved me from looking ridiculous.

Respond to constructive criticism by asking yourself if possibly he knows something that you don't know. If he says you are being overbearing and pushy by insisting the two of you take that trip down the Amazon, do an about face and say that you are willing to first try mosquito season in New Jersey to see what that South American holiday might be like. When you are wrong about something admit it and apologize. Don't scream "You always abuse me" to the point that you become abusive yourself. Instead say "I hear you and I see what I did wrong and how it must make you feel."

Don't play the blame game in order to reduce your own internal guilt. Scratch this and other forms of self-defense and take on responsibility in those situations where you have contributed to a problem. Sew what you rip. If you broke it, be sure to fix it. When Santiago comes home, he complains about how closed-in the house seems. Jessie interprets that as a sign that Santiago isn't happy to be home. But the house is really stuffy and Jessie, having been home all day, has simply gotten used to it. Jessie was tempted to ask Santiago to stop criticizing him until he realized that a better solution would have been to just open the windows. Let him win ones like this. Winning stops struggles cold and as an extra bonus it gets you the sympathy vote, kudos for being empathic, admiration for getting real, and self-congratulations for being such a nice guy.

Of course, apologizing doesn't mean flogging yourself. Just take the blame on yourself in a quiet, subtle, and noninvasive way. For example, when there is a misunderstanding, instead of all the mea culpas let it be known that you recognize that the problem is that you didn't make yourself clear.

Consult with him

To avoid making him feel invisible or swamped by your strong personality, consult with him before making really important decisions about such things as decorating, socializing, and spending money. Always make sure, before you complete a business transaction with a third party, that you have first cleared it with him.

Subscribe to old-fashioned values and follow the classic rules of etiquette

Scratch any husband and you find that man with the pitchfork in the classic painting *American Gothic*. So get out there, stop being a Scene Queen, drop that drag, don those overalls, grab that farm tool, and this very day start developing a touch of local color about you. Get ready to have the greatest relationship of the nineteenth century. Don't listen to the gurus with all those modern notions who think that there are fashions in human nature, which therefore changes with the calendar. Love is an old pair of underwear, tattered but true, one you want to keep wearing even when it has holes in it because its label finally went soft and stopped giving you a fit. If you really want that Donna Reed style of relationship, don't begin to fear conformity after listening to friends who tell you, "Home by five and to bed by ten just isn't outlandish enough to cut it." Decide if it is more "you" to put that ring in your nose or on your finger. Try not to act up just to avoid being bourgeois, making your life's goal hitting the conservatives in the midriff. Instead hearken back to old times when marriage consisted of the corny values of honesty, commitment, trust, and respect—oldies but goodies that are still very much up to date, and still form the cornerstone of solid, lasting relationships, gay or straight.

Always be honest

Being dishonest even in one small thing can completely lose you respect in your husband's eyes, and additionally make him suspicious of everything else that you say and do. It's better to confess something and be temporarily embarrassed about it than to hide something and get caught at it. Here is a guideline. Never do anything you wouldn't want him to find out about, but if you *do* do something of that nature, make sure he finds out about it, *fast,* and from you first.

Always say something; don't fall silent for prolonged periods of time

Always say something back when he says something to you, even when you don't have much to add. Being silent leaves room for many interpretations, most of them unfavorable. It makes you not an inscrutable character whose still waters run deep but a walking Rorschach blot that virtually begs for a misinterpretation, and that usually along negative lines, not "Darling, I see a dancing bear in those pretty little ink blots," but "Looks to me like a picture of a snappy little vagina with a tiny but sharp row of fangs inside plotting to take another little ding out of my dong."

Don't make jokes at his expense

Every time Larry could not find a CD of his, he would ask Josh if he borrowed it and forgot to return it, a joke since Josh would never want one of Larry's obscure contemporary music extravaganzas. At first Josh would laugh at the joke, but then he would begin to think that Larry was accusing him of borrowing his things and not returning them. It reminded Josh of an off-putting loaded question a neighbor once asked him: "Did you walk off by mistake with my faux-diamond necklace?" Teasing and sarcasm in the form of little digs and subtle putdowns, funny or no, have no place in a relationship. In fact they can be the most devastating of all, because the victim cannot prove intent and instead thinks he is just being oversensitive.

Once Marty, trying to rescue a snapping turtle from the yard, asked Roger to help. Roger said that he was afraid it would charge him, to which Marty replied, "It's only a turtle; how much can it charge?" Roger got paranoid and read that as a put-down of his silly fears though it was mainly an innocent joke.

Interrupt vicious cycles

Vicious cycles typically start small. They might start with a funny blaming look that leads to a defensive response that leads to counter-retaliation. Or they might start with a little misunderstanding. Tim asked Dan if he drank milk. Dan said no, then Tim asked, "So where are you getting your calcium?" Dan then said, "Who cares?" Tim thought Dan meant "Lay off, bitch" when he actually meant, "I don't worry about that, I'm still young, my bones won't break." So Tim felt put-down and unloved and instead of recognizing that he was being hypersensitive blamed Dan for being hypercritical. So he decided, "I'm not getting love at home," and went out to get it elsewhere.

Or these cycles might start with a minor personality clash or with a button being pushed. Maybe you hate being told what to do because you have trouble distinguishing a legitimate request or a good suggestion from an unwelcome command and he knows this but continues to try to control you. Maybe you are a bit stubborn and like to do the opposite of what he asks you to do and he constantly demands this and that even though he knows that it makes you frantic. Maybe you are very laid back and he insists on being a perfectionist, or a man of too many principles who always has to determine for sure "who is right" and "who is wrong" when it's not really that important. Maybe you need to be dominant and he insists on being right all the time. Once Harold said that from the look of things they are still clipping dogs' tails these days even though it hurts the dogs, to which Roger responded, pointing out a dog with an unclipped tail, "No, they stopped," but an argument started. Maybe you are too neat and he refuses to stop being just a little too sloppy. Russell followed Stan around the house, picking up after him all the way. That made Stan mad so he said, "Can't you just let a little mess be there for two minutes?" Still Russell wouldn't quit until Stan, inspired to retaliate, dropped things on the floor just to watch Russell get annoyed and pick them up, which inspired Russell to call Stan a slob, and you know the rest.

A good way to avoid vicious cycles characterized by progressively escalating anger is to accept his minor annoyances with you. If you fight back he will insist he is right and you are wrong, and there you go. But if you instead say, "I understand how you feel and I take some of the blame for your feeling that way," he is likely to calm down almost immediately. Or just act as if his anger doesn't matter that much to you. I will always remember an incident when I got into an uproar about something really dumb. Michael didn't get into an uproar back. Instead he just sat on the sofa and patted the cushions, asking me to sit down so he could rub my back. The End. If you are the angry one, try to remember that when you have anger on your mind, your mind is a terrific thing to waste.

A good way to interrupt vicious cycles is to just try having sex. Some people fight to avoid having sex. I suggest you look into the possibility of having sex to avoid fighting.

Set appropriate limits (just say no)

Positivity is not all sweetness and light. Sometimes positivity involves setting limits for his own good and for the good of your relationship. Of course these limits have to be set without nagging and haranguing, and they have to be both sensible and justified, not just an overflow product of a strong personality with a strong will, meaning that you always have to be in control, no matter what.

Saying no and otherwise setting limits is a particularly good idea with partners who equate your telling them to stop with your telling them you love them. It also might be a good idea when: he is cheating on you; he is abusing you verbally; he threatens you with bodily harm; he takes drugs; he drinks excessively; he says he wants an open relationship and you don't; he is frequently away from home, for a long time and not for a great reason; he is too clingy and dependent and excessively demanding; he is seriously controlling; he is seriously provocative to get you to be the one to blow up so that he doesn't have to take responsibility for starting something; or he seriously deprives you of something important that you want and should have, like when Tripp left Richard in the middle of a severe case of flu to keep a lunch date with his mother so that they could discuss her purchasing a new lounge chair.

Todd once asked Chris to get him a document they both needed. Then when he didn't get it for a month and a half he asked him again only to get a snippy reply that "the problem isn't my not getting you the document, the problem is your being too impatient." Todd tried to be more patient, only Chris continued to stall. So instead of remaining patient Todd decided to become petulant. After the first "dammit" Chris got him the document and now Todd is happy because he got what he wanted, and so is Chris, because he feels less guilty about withholding something that Todd needed.

Effectively setting limits starts with being clear about what you want and passing that on precisely. Garbled messages confuse everybody and he certainly cannot read your mind, so don't say something half way because you are afraid of speaking up at all. Sol never liked Wilfredo's dog much. He hated her constant barking when people came over to the house or when Sol was trying to work. Now Sol wants another dog but Wilfredo won't let him have it because he yelled constantly at the last one, and Wilfredo is certain that that is indicative of how he treats all dogs, even the quiet ones. Sol thinks that's not fair, but he doesn't ask Wilfredo to reconsider. Instead he seethes with resentment and drips big hints about not being understood. Then one day he blows up, screaming about how Wilfredo is a lousy companion, and that between the two of them he would much prefer the dog.

Setting limits does not work well with all partners. It works well with partners who are capable of feeling guilt (not all men are); with partners who are masochistic enough to want "no" for an answer and self-punitive enough to seek punishment for their transgressions; and with partners who like you butch and in charge. It doesn't work well with impulsive partners who don't listen; partners addicted to punishment who just want, need, and beg for a masochistic fix; sadistic partners who really hate and want to hurt you; or obsessive partners who can't make up their minds and act decisively about anything. And of course don't set limits when there is nothing really important going on, and certainly don't attempt to straightjacket him when you are the one who is acting crazy.

Be 100 percent faithful to your partner

Make your lover all, not just part, of your life. Don't make a sexual "arrangement" if you are doing so because you fear intimacy, so that your arrangement is an uncaring hostile way to say, "I love you, but don't rely on it, because I don't love you all the way, or at least not like that."

Always put on a good show

Always be the best that you can be. Cultivate your talents and your appearance—and do it not just for you but also for him so that he will find you interesting and be proud of you. Don't let yourself go then rail at him, "Whatsamatter; are you ashamed of me?" Instead ask yourself if he has reason to cringe when the two of you appear in public, and if so, try to start looking and behaving in a way that does him proud. Do a serious self-check, look for little hints about what he wants you to be, and comply, yield, and give in when he is making at least a little sense. Is he looking around at slim young men? You might not be able to become younger, but you sure can become thinner.

Adjust your expectations of your relationship

Expect the right amount from your relationship—not too little and not too much. If you settle for too little, that is exactly what you will get. Some of the imperfections of some relationships can be fixed and you should at least try. But don't expect too much from your relationship either. No relationship is ideal, and not all relationship problems can be solved. Accept that there will be small problems in your relationship and just don't let them make too big a dent in your overall happiness. All lovers make mistakes and have bad days. That is not important. It really doesn't matter in the infinite scheme of things that he invites someone over for dinner without checking with you first, any more than it really matters that the woman in front of you on the line in the supermarket is going through with one more than the allowed number of items.

Try to help him improve, but don't give up on him completely if you can't. See him as a whole person. To do that, make a list of both his vices and his virtues so that you can decide what predominates. Your list should have two columns on the page. In the left column of the list write down the evil your man does, and on the right column of the list write down the good, and if you are being honest you will almost certainly see that the good side is longer than the bad. As always, rate the importance of each item on your list by giving it one to five spaces depending on its inherent significance to you in the here and now and its ultimate importance in the grand and infinite scheme of things. One line is trivial, five lines is important. This way you can weigh the items not only according to how numerous they are but also according to how much space they do, or should, occupy on the page, and so in your life.

Be trusting

Trust takes time to develop. In the beginning, do trust, but do be careful. Don't do anything irreversible too soon, like move in with someone you hardly know when you can't move out again, or turn over all your finances to someone who may be dishonest. Hold back turning your emotions over too, but don't lose him by closing up all your feelings. Remember that your suspicion creates his dishonesty. Cheaters often cheat because they are doing what is expected of them. I have too often heard the rough equivalent of "He is going to accuse me of doing it no matter what, so I might as well have a grand parade if I am going to get rained on no matter what I do."

Be patient

The tincture of time can be the best healer of them all. So give your marriage a chance by giving yourself enough time to get through the rough spots that are always present in any relationship. Never panic thinking that just because things aren't great today it means that they will not get better tomorrow. Don't by rushing to judgment make your relationship all beginning and end with no middle. Many relationship problems burn out spontaneously, or if they don't they at least become old fast. Things that bother you today often do not bother you tomorrow. What's missing from your relationship now can develop later. Many problem marriages settle down in time and many childish lovers of today grow up and become loving adults of tomorrow.

Be toxin-free

Do not smoke too much of the bad stuff. I recommend relative sobriety when it comes to alcohol, too. It makes you more appealing, you'll have fewer wrinkles, and you have your emotions under better control so that you don't say or do any of those horrible things that people say and do when they get smashed.

Be predictable

Always be someone he can count on. Never throw him off balance by being nice to him one day then turning on him the next.

In summary

A summary of the positive-affirmative approach to marriage would include:

- Making marriage your number-one priority.
- Recognizing that you don't matter nearly as much as your relationship does.
- Identifying destructive patterns and replacing them with constructive, corrective ones.
- Deferring to him when he feels more strongly than you and is more anxious about something than you are.
- Accommodating by understanding and putting his needs first, and yours second.
- Being sympathetic. Understanding when he is hurting because things are emotionally or realistically difficult for him then either trying to help him out or backing off until he can get himself together.
- Making small changes in you in the realization that they have big implications for him—and for the both of you.
- Helping him change by treating him right, for example by developing positive characteristics, and by being Mr. Nice Guy.
- Humoring him when he is a little out of sorts and out of line.
- Accepting his constructive criticism of you and changing for the better when necessary.
- Setting tough-love limits on him when that is what he needs.
- Interrupting vicious cycles of being a bitch who gets bitched then becomes bitchier and bitches even more.
- Never giving up on your relationship prematurely but instead giving it chance to grow, stabilize, and heal.
- Being patient, remembering that in marriage as in life if you wait

long enough, many stop signals simply turn to go.

The next chapters focus on the common Danger Zones that plague gay relationships. Not much damage is done when partners go into and out of these zones temporarily and only on occasion; however, a lot of bad things happen when partners go into and stay in one or several of these zones for prolonged periods of time.

5

Danger Zone 1: Overcoming Boredom and Restlessness

Gay men who become bored and restless feel uninterested in what is a perfectly good relationship with a perfectly interesting partner. The pressure builds to move on and either have new and therefore presumably more exciting sexual experiences or to prematurely break up what could at least potentially have been a wonderful long-term committed relationship leading to a lifetime of happiness.

You are in the bored and restless zone if you check off more than half of the following items as being strongly applicable to you.

- I have lost interest in him because he has gotten old fast—both figuratively and literally.
- I feel a sense of aching dullness, as if every day with him is the same-old, same-old tired experience.
- I often get desperate for a little variety and change.
- My relationship is like living in a bad climate, and I can no longer stand the rain, roast, rime, and refrigeration.
- I know down deep that I get enough of everything I need at home, but I still want more.
- I know down deep that things are good at home, but I still want better.
- I demand more fun out of my life.

- I demand more life out of my fun.
- Our sex life was great in the beginning, but now it has become routine and predictable.
- I miss the wonderful roller-coaster thrills of the chase and the conquest.
- I want to put more risk in my life so that I can reexperience the excitement and danger I used to know.
- I miss the joy of making new discoveries in new bodies.
- I only feel really like myself when I am having sex with someone new.
- When cruising for someone new, I tend to forget about all those terrible letdowns and disappointments where all I could salvage afterwards was hope for better luck next time.
- I actively knock him so that I can give myself a reason to become interested in someone else.
- Marriage isn't right for everybody, especially everybody gay.
- I think I would be much better off single, being able to come and go as I please.
- Cheating is a man thing.
- Polygamy is the essence of being gay. What good is it to be proud that you are gay if you don't regularly do something to prove it to yourself and to the world.
- I have a bunch of friends who agree with me that one man is not quite enough. They are the ones I am going to consult when I finally decide to make my break.

Believe it or not, in long-term relationships a little boredom is actually a good thing—not a cause for alarm, but a reason for rejoicing. For, just as being a little hungry is a sign that your diet is on track, being a little bored is a sign that your relationship is working. That's because long-term relationships are not meant to be constantly exciting. They are working romances meant to be more like a planet than like an asteroid—

bigger than life, solid as a rock, and predictable in orbit. In fact, in a sense, boredom is actually a positive experience because it is relaxing, lulling, and quietly reassuring. It means that there isn't much tension in your relationship. In a way then, if you feel a little bored with your lover, it could very well mean that you are truly happy with him.

Too much boredom, however, is not a good thing. It suggests one of two possibilities. Too much boredom may mean that your partner is a really uninteresting, truly unsatisfactory type of guy, just plain wrong either for you or for almost everyone. Or, and this is perhaps the most common scenario, it may mean that you are thinking negatively about a positive situation, and you are doing that for purely emotional reasons. If the latter is the case, don't even think of exchanging an old partner for a new one. Don't seek out amusements and diversions like tight blue jeans, sultry surroundings, sexy music, candlelight dinners, or sex toys to revive your sex life. Instead try handling the emotional impediments that are keeping you from flying, both literally and figuratively. Here are some possibilities. See if any of these apply to you, and if they do, make sure you make the implied corrections.

You are overplaying the importance of his looks because you need someone to show off more than you need someone to love. Yes, it never hurts to have a good-looking man, but sometimes not wearing well can be a quality shared by partners who are only handsome and jeans that are only designer.

You are mistakenly expecting sex to stay exactly the same forever. But sex does change over time. However, that doesn't mean that it gets boring. It just becomes different. It flattens and broadens out, its original qualities transformed into new ones that develop, amplify, and improve on the old experience, so that while sex gets tamer at the same time it paradoxically gets wilder. When that happens it just means that you are getting comfortable with sex. Don't confuse that with getting bored with it.

You are expressing feelings of aggravation and anger. The feelings "I am bored with you," and "I feel restless in my relationship" often really mean not "I am tired of you," but "I am mad at you."

You feel sheepish about loving. Many gay men feel guilty about loving due to a fear of closeness, intimacy, and commitment. If this is you, when you should be looking upon closeness as a wonderful thing, you instead see it as a trap you just have to escape from. So you actually arrange to feel bored because that way you can convince yourself that you are not getting too close, and you want to feel restless and think about having new experiences because that way you can reassure yourself that you are not getting too comfortable with the old. You actually look for reasons to flee your relationship because that way you can reassure yourself that the desire to flee is not your poison but your antidote.

You are struggling with feelings of self-hatred. You might be one of those gay men who dislikes himself too much to let himself have fun, or, if you are having fun, to acknowledge that you are. So you welcome being bored because it reassures you that you aren't enjoying yourself too much, that is, more than you believe you by rights ought to be.

Your self-esteem is low. You feel that your relationship cannot be any good just because it's yours.

You are addicted to thrills. Like a gambler, you only feel high when you win, and you only feel that you have won when you have scored. Only now do you feel powerful, in control of the world, favored by fate and God, gifted in both a literal and figurative sense, and up to any challenge that might come your way. Only now are you able to convince yourself that you are not a big nobody who is the passive victim of forces beyond your control, but are instead a big somebody because you can actively beat the odds even when they are overwhelmingly against you, making you a mover of the earth rather than a passive victim of an earthquake.

You feel depressed. Though you are living the champagne life, you nevertheless feel you are living on a beer budget.

Your pinkness is tinged with the green of envy. You think that everyone has more than you do, and what they have is better than what you have. You feel like a big loser because your guy isn't a big, big, big winner.

You confuse your partner with your parent. Having parentalized your partner, you feel stuck at home with him now as you once felt stuck with your parents, and you would kill to get out of anything now that even distantly resembles that earlier straitjacket. You even begin to imagine that that accepting partner of yours is, just like your mother, your worst critic, an evil eye always watching you, a harpy from hell always putting you down.

You buy into what gay society says about gay relationships, as if what's current is also invariably right on the money. You, like a lot of gay men, let yourself be convinced that a good marriage requires a hot romance. But romance is one of the things that taste just as good, or even better, when served at room temperature.

Michael and I spend hours wandering around stores looking for food freebies and pseudo-bargains. The thought never crosses my mind that we should be doing something more exciting with our lives. What crosses my mind is other, *better*, thoughts, like "Look where you would be without him" and "What you are doing in the low-cost warehouse is really so much better for you and so much more fun than what you could be doing in the really high-cost bushes, bars, and baths."

Here are some good ways to emerge from this particular danger zone.

Rev up your interest in your guy. One way to do that is to get to know him better. Start by learning the fascinating things that you might not already know about him, things that we all tend to forget when we have been around someone for a long time. Try to discover what is going on in that cute little head of his. You might be amazed, startled, and moved, and, while this isn't always a good thing, if you are a thrill-seeker you might even be pleasantly surprised to discover that you are taking more risks with him than you previously thought.

Push yourself to get close to him. Force yourself to spend as much time with him as you possibly can. Never let him out of your sight. It might even make sense to move with him from the city to a more rural area where there are fewer distractions. Rather than complain that you are too clingy, he just might be flattered by all the closeness, and might, perhaps after a few rough moments, come to like this new level of intensity in your relationship and wind up so lovingly involved with you that it won't be possible for you any longer to think of him as dull.

Have lots of sex all the time with him hoping to make it a habit, while also tiring yourself out until you are just too exhausted to feel much like looking for someone else. Become a slut not only in the bedroom but all over the house. Grab his crotch every time he walks by and wherever you are. Follow my basic principle for keeping sex alive: abuse it, and you won't lose it.

Learn to live with being bored and restless. Do the same thing per- formers do to cope with stage fright they cannot entirely master: accept and work around it. Build your boredom and restlessness into your acceptable displeasure quotient, alongside such things as being in a coma when you first get up in the morning, being hungry when you are on a diet, having to stay awake until the five o'clock bell rings at work, having to say no to that drink, cigarette, or patisserie, and the other bad feelings we all have to accept in life because squelching them takes too much effort, involves more pain than it's worth, or is just impossible to do anyway.

Meanwhile, keep your boredom and restlessness a secret from him. I believe in honesty between people, but only up to a point. It is insulting, hurtful, and disappointing for him to learn that your eye is roving and that your attention is wandering. I don't believe in hiding affairs because I don't believe in having them in the first place. But I do believe in hiding fantasies because you cannot help having those. Even when they are not necessarily a positional statement, should they come out they can look like one and hurt. Many gay men I know have dreams of infidelity and there is nothing much to be done about them—except to have sex often enough with your partner so that they are both dry and infrequent. But when your lover asks you what you were dreaming about last night, if it is a revealing dream, tell him you dreamt that you were running in place, not away from him. You don't want to be unfaithful. You really do want to be faithful, you just cannot help your unfaithful biology from surfacing every now and then. So you are not lying, you are just refusing to let your hormones do your talking for you.

Here is just the wrong remedy: You may not be able to stop having waking fantasies of other partners, but you should never do what some gurus advocate and actively encourage yourself to think of someone else while having sex with your guy. This may work today, but ultimately it only brings about dissatisfaction and gives you more to be restless about tomorrow. It can also develop into a bad habit as you condition yourself until the only way you can get excited is by thinking about other men. That can eventually lead to poorer sexual performance with him, which of course in the long run can create even more boredom and restlessness for both of you.

More specific ways out of the boredom and restlessness zone are discussed in the individual chapters applicable to the specific causes of boredom and restlessness. For example, the remedy for boredom and restlessness due to anger is discussed in chapter 7.

Perhaps it is not you but your partner who complains of being bored and restless. Now you have a different job to do. You have to help him revive his flagging interest and calm his agitation down.

Step one involves getting in touch with his needs and desires. Don't criticize him for being dissatisfied. Instead accept his dissatisfaction, find out what it is all about, and give him what he wants, based on the principle that it's hard to get bored with someone who is constantly trying to gratify you. Really go into things here. Did you ask him if was okay for you to screw around and he said yes? Is it possible that he said "yes" when he really meant to say "no"? So before you accept "yes" as an answer, ask yourself how many times you asked him, and if he said "yes" why did he say that? Because he is a masochist? Because he felt threatened by you in some significant way, for example because he feels you will leave him if he says it is not okay? If these things are true, the only answer you should accept to the question, "Is it okay for me to screw around?" is "no."

Step two involves not doing the things I list throughout that might turn him off. To summarize and anticipate, don't be a chronic pain in the ass or a bring-you-down pessimist—a cloud without a sky. Don't be a neat freak who has to cut a hole in a doily and put it around his thing before you even deign to touch it. Don't have the narrow horizons of someone who has nothing better to talk about at six thirty than what they said on the six o'clock news. And while style isn't the most important thing, people do walk out when messes walk in. Just recently a member of my family complained that her husband, while watching TV, was reading a girl-group's logo emblazoned on their T-shirts. She bitched that he was secretly looking at their tits. Maybe he was, and maybe he was doing that because she had let herself go physically then made matters worse by wearing ill-fitting clothes from Second Hand Rose. If this is you, listen to cues from him about how he wants you to look and act and dress as nicely, and behave as well, as you possibly can, doing so for him, not for fashion or to be socially correct. Does he like you clean-shaven or unshaven? If clean-shaven, forget that stubble. Does he think your T-shirts are too large or too much like a tourniquet? Another place where size counts. Does he like to show you off but seethe with resentment because you aren't giving him something nice to put on display? Don't buy cheap stuff at the discount stores and don't deliberately cultivate that frugal and shoddy look to tell him and the world that financially you are into budgeting and philosophically all about reverse chic.

Get regular physicals so that you stay healthy for him, as well as for yourself. Maintain your weight by not eating too much junk food. Do not smoke or drink to excess. Do not do bizarre things to your appearance like going to extremes to reverse hair loss or the aging process. Maybe you feel that a toupee or a comb-over is alluring, but maybe he hates it and is too shy or too polite to say anything. Stand in front of the mirror and decide if your reflection could use some serious reflecting.

Most of all, do what you can to gain his respect. I never get bored with Michael because I respect him, and I respect him because he earns my respect by being faithful, caring, and hardworking. He is, above all, solid. As a result, getting bored and restless with a guy like The Michael is as impossible as getting bored and restless with an encyclopedia like The Britannica.

6

Danger Zone 2: Curing Sexual Problems—Sexual Inhibition, Sexual Addiction, and Cheating; and Dealing with Polygamy

This chapter contains two checklists. The first is meant to help you determine if you are sexually inhibited, and the second if you are sexually addicted. It's a heads up if you answer yes to even one of the questions in the first (sexually inhibited) checklist, or to two of the questions in the second (sexually addicted, or "sexaholic") checklist. Self knowledge in these areas is pivotal for understanding cheating, mastering the compulsion to be polygamous, and moving on to monogamy if that is your true goal but one which you have not as yet been able to achieve.

The sexually inhibited zone

- Sex isn't important; comfort is all that counts.
- I don't mind if he has a misteress; shopping is more interesting than sex.
- Sometimes I feel that sex is not lofty or spiritual but dirty and animalistic.
- It hurts when I do it because I cannot relax.
- I can't come no matter what he does to me.
- I can only come when I masturbate myself.

- I get an erection okay but I quickly lose it.
- I come too quickly, I think sometimes just to get it over with.
- Though I am unable to perform satisfactorily with my partner, it works fine with almost everyone else.
- I quickly lose interest in someone who gets seriously interested in me—certainly my partner, but also every new man I meet.

The sexaholic zone

- I think about sex all the time.
- No one guy, and especially him, can meet all my sexual needs.
- I tend to fall madly in love with men I hardly know, then afterwards I can't think what I had in mind at the time.
- It's true when they say that when it comes to gay sex one man is not quite enough.
- I am a very seductive individual, a tease and a flirt with anyone good-looking.
- I feel driven to check out what every cute man I meet has "down there." Once I satisfy my curiosity, I move on to check out what the next man has.
- It's a good thing that we have an arrangement that allows us to have outside experiences and occasional threesomes. Otherwise I would feel constantly deprived and frustrated.
- I feel that I only come alive when I am in love with someone new.
- I feel that I only come alive when I am having sex with someone new. Sex with a series of partners is the only thing that makes me feel "with it" enough to feel good about myself, and to feel whole.
- I go on to the next partner because I feel that there is something not just right about the last one—for example, his legs aren't the right size, or they just don't have enough hair on them for me.
- When I am able to attract cute strangers, I feel strong, worthwhile,

beautiful, admired, and loved.

- Sometimes I think that I run around just so that I don't have to look inside and face the pain in my heart. It's hard to get depressed when you are on a sexual high.
- I sometimes look back on my life and think that I made major life decisions not on the basis of what would get me paid but on the basis of what would get me laid.

Some people buy into the proposition that all gay men are sluts at heart, and that cheating and polygamy (defined below) trace the essence of being gay. I disagree, and instead suggest that fidelity to a partner is commoner than we think, and cheating on a partner is rarer than many gay men and the straight and gay media suggest. Too many of the relevant statistics are anomalous because they don't take into account the large group of invisible gay men who love both wisely and well—at home, silently, and behind closed doors, too content to worry about being counted.

As I emphasize throughout this book, I strongly believe that gay (and straight) marriage should be strictly monogamous—that is, no cheating, and no arrangements. This is a philosophy that won't appeal to everybody, but it works for me, and I believe that it will be good for you. Indeed, I feel that monogamy is the true and only way to make gay marriage really work and last. Sure, many gay men cheat and are polygamous yet stay together for a lifetime. But that doesn't make that the best of all possible arrangements. If you don't buy that, okay, fine. If you think my standards are wrong-headed and inflexible and that I am the bearer of unbearable inhibitions, fine too. Either modify my suggestions to suit your personal orientation or disregard them entirely. But at least try to see where I am coming from and if my viewpoint has as much in it for you as it does for me, and makes as much sense for your relationship as it does for mine.

Cheating

As I define it, cheating differs from polygamy. Polygamy is an arrangement, cheating is a derangement. Polygamy is a lifestyle choice, that is, an above-board satisfactory and mutually satisfying working arrangement where both partners are in on what's going on and agree to do and accept it without too many reservations. In contrast, cheating is almost always as much a below-the-table lie as it is a below-the-belt behavior. Partners who cheat make contracts together then break them separately, and behind each other's backs. That makes them basically immoral individuals. The only time that morality enters into cheating is when the participants get guilty afterwards, and most cheaters wait to do that until the sex is over and it's too late to return it. Now they put their lover back on first base, but only, of course, after they have scored.

Just recently I spoke to Rudolfo, one of my patients. He was still crying about how upset he was that ten years ago he worked double shifts to support his household with Phil, his partner at the time, only later to discover that Phil had sent him off to work two jobs so that he could get him out of the house so that he could use the place to see someone he was having regular sex with on the side. Like many cheaters, Phil made different rules for sex than he made for everything else. He accepted, and expected Rudolfo to accept, behavior in the sexual arena that he wouldn't even consider outside of it. As he himself admitted, "If I treated my clients at work the way I treat my husband at home, I would both have no marriage and be out of a job."

Cheaters aren't always having as much fun as you might think. That's because down deep they feel guilty about their cheating. They tend to deal with their guilt with a series of rationalizations like the ones I discuss below. But if you are in the cheating zone, no matter how you rationalize your cheating, cheating remains not sex but sex on the sly, and it isn't any less morally wrong or deceitful just because it's sexual slyness as distinct from the other kinds, like slyly cheating on your taxes, or slyly putting a can or two from the supermarket shelf in your pocket.

Speaking from experience, I have never treated a couple whose cheating has not been divisive. While polygamous partners often stay together, cheating partners typically grow further and further apart. Their relationship is marred by constant fights, recriminations, guilty confessions, and tearful promises to reform, with much of their professed guilt, if any, though it looks real, just a smoke screen for business as usual.

So, if you are cheating on your husband, **step one** involves seriously considering ceasing and desisting, and doing so now, before it's too late. It helps to give some serious thought to the potential consequences of your cheating. So often a moment's pleasure means a lifetime of pain, with triple trouble. First you get guilty, then you get rejected, then you get ejected. Is my patient's tale of woe your story too? "Jack and I finally broke up after eight years. He came out late in life, and I respect his wanting to try new things, but I told him, 'You don't expect me to stay home while you run around, do you?' So I did run around, then I left, and now he is begging me to come back, and I won't do it, I'm too happy the way things are now. Also I enjoy every minute of my new life even more because I know I am fixing him for what he did to me in the old one."

Step two involves asking yourself not *if*, but *how much*, your cheating is hurting him. In my experience partners of men who cheat get very emotional about their lovers doing it with other men. They might say, "It doesn't bother me," but I have discovered that that is almost always a cover-up for how they really feel. There is every reason to believe that many gay men have strong feelings about being cuckolded, and, believe it or not, sometimes the feelings are even stronger than they are with straight men.

Step three consists of having a quiet session of honest self-exploration where you ask yourself, "Why am I doing this?" Once you find out, and understand your cheating through and through, you are more likely to see the need to change your mind and discover the way to change your behavior. Here are some possibilities for you to consider to explain your behavior so that you can clean up your act:

Is it because you want to hurt him? Frequently gay men cheat not for the sex but to be mean and hurtful to their partners. When cheaters get caught, as they frequently do, it is so often because they want to get caught. The real payoff for the cheating is not the sex but their partner's negative response when he finds out about it, which they make certain he does. That's why when gay men who are cheating tell me that they regret having destroyed their marriages, I always ask them whether they are revealing their response to events they set in motion or confessing the true nature of their original intent.

Ask yourself, if you are self-homophobic. You are feeling guilty about being gay, and you find your guilt intensifies when you become very serious about a given relationship, so you cope by seeking out partners who are devalued because they are anonymous or otherwise lack emotional significance for you. As a bonus, you avoid devaluing your little angel, the one you put up on a pedestal that is a bit too high for anyone to comfortably perch on. Yours is figuratively a "my saintly mother didn't do it" view of human sexuality in general and of your partner's homosexuality in particular. So you graciously avoid "contaminating" him by only having sex with other men, and you pick rough trade types because you feel that they are already so devalued that they (and you) have nothing to lose. Probably you are congratulating yourself for differentiating saintly *him* from trashy *them*. Paradoxically, then, for you cheating is a sign of your love for him. Of course, as you have already guessed, he won't see it that way, so my advice to you is to right now start loving him better by starting to live under another sign.

Maybe you are desperately seeking a parent—someone to care for you like your real mother did, or someone to care for you like your real mother didn't, or someone strong and handsome like your father was, or someone strong and handsome like your father wasn't. Next, unless your man meets those criteria precisely, or unless you can at least view him as someone who meets those criteria exactly, you lose interest in him first personally then sexually, and off you go in a new and futile search for a substitute which, like anything else that is only a substitute, never fully satisfies.

Maybe you are a very showoffy kind of person, who, needing to act wild and in an exhibitionistic fashion, cheats to be noticed and thought of as cool. For you, monogamy is uncool because it is just too square and moral, and what kind of a she-devil are you if you never do anything even slightly satanic? Yielding to peer and social pressure to keep your distance is your way to please and keep your friends.

Do you feel resentful and vengeful toward him because of something that he did and are withholding love because you just can't forgive him for it? Why can't you become more forgiving and start adoring him more? That showing love works is illustrated by my relationship with Buster, my neighbor's guard mutt. Buster used to be a growler who started in on me whenever I tried to get near him or his mistress. The way to stop him from growling, she told us, was to call him by name and say, over and over again, "Good dog, good dog, I love you." It worked. The growling stopped and the tail started wagging. Why should it be any different with your man? When he growls, call him by name, say you love him, and watch it start wagging, where it counts.

Ask yourself if you fear becoming intimate, and if you fear that because you fear having your feelings hurt by a man whom you suspect is going to reject you, so you are trying to save yourself by refusing to put all your eggs in his basket.

Perhaps you can't enjoy your relationship fully because you can't enjoy most things due to guilt about having fun of any sort. Some people cannot enjoy an activity just because it's the kind of activity that they should give up. But you give up an activity just because it's the kind of activity you enjoy. If this is you, you may be deliberately screwing up your relationship and with it your sex just so you don't get too much satisfaction out of life. I think of the guy who told me that his mother offered to buy him any kind of ice-cream except chocolate. But, as his mother knew, that was the only kind he liked. Now my friend found himself in the position of either paying himself for something he liked or of getting something for free that he hated. Why did his mother come up with this big idea? Because his mother knew that a particular chocolate ice-cream tasted the best, and thought that while feeding yourself a little (compromised) pleasure was okay, it was a sin to enjoy yourself to the max.

You could be a serious masochist. With you, like the legendary lemming, it's a case of "Show me a cliff and I'll show you a hundred-yard dash." Or, maybe you are so afraid of control that you even confuse controlling yourself with submitting to tyranny.

Or you could be a very selfish person who refuses to deprive yourself of anything good, and your morality is cut from that sinister tube where you don't much care what your partner thinks. You just do what gets you what you want, without much concern for how he might feel about it. If this is you, you don't criticize yourself for cheating. Instead you come up with lots of effective fashionable distortive rationalizations to prove it is perfectly okay to cheat.

Here are some of the ones I hear most frequently:

• I am too young to settle down just yet.

- I got married before I had a chance to sample what's out there so it's too soon for me to commit to only one man.
- Cheating is the essence of being gay.
- Everyone is doing it.
- He does it too.
- He did it first.
- He wouldn't mind because it's only sex, and having sex with someone else doesn't mean I don't love him.
- I never see the same man twice.
- We only do mutual masturbation and that's not really having sex.

Generally good at subtle, self-serving illogic, you give the lie to the aphorism that you cannot fool all the people all the time. You know all the loopholes, have the best excuses, and know how to use preexisting moral uncertainty for personal gain. Your best port in your personal storm is that not all gay men agree that monogamy is a great idea. Of course, it doesn't hurt that you also know how to cover your tracks to make sure your partner can't figure out where exactly you are heading. So if he has a discussion with you about what's happening, you simply lie to him. You mess with his head more or less the same way that you mess with the rules. From you he won't hear contrition, but will instead hear "Whatsamatter; don't you trust me?" accompanied by flowing crocodile tears. You are also terrific at getting third parties to aid you in your cheating by running cover for you and offering you their apartment to do it in, then, when you get caught, to take your side, and give you solace and absolution along the lines of "Anyone in your shoes would do exactly the same thing."

If your partner is cheating on you, and you want to rescue your marriage rather than make his cheating grounds for your divorce, **step one** involves developing basic distrust. Don't believe much of anything he says. Be like a parole officer and check up on him constantly and do whatever is necessary to put a stop to his behavior. Especially if yours is a partner who married you for your money/family/name/apartment and is looking to get divorced just so that he can clean you out, what your marriage might need in addition to a therapist is a battery of detectives and lawyers, and sometimes, if only figuratively, a trip to the vet to put a tracking device under his skin.

Step two involves just asking him to stop it and instead to become more honest, trustworthy, and faithful. But don't whine, "Please don't do this to me." Instead gain his respect by acting from a position of strength. Extract the promise from him that he will change and get him to agree to allow you to monitor his progress without his complaining that you are distrustful, or calling you paranoid.

Step three involves asking yourself if you are somehow contributing to the problem. Are you letting your appearance go? Be honest about this, and if so make the necessary changes. Carry yourself well, be neat and clean, dress pleasantly, and cover up the dark side of your physicality by keeping it private between you and you. For example, hide any physical flaws under the nicest clothes you can find. Also stop mistreating him emotionally if you are doing that in any way. Are you putting him down? Put him down and he won't want to do it with you, won't be able to do it with you, and won't care that he hasn't done it with you for months or years. Next you will love him less, and feel less like holding and embracing him. He will experience that as a further put-down, and cheat even more to repair his injured and damaged self, becoming fascinated with new people because you drove him to explore the world to reassure himself that at least someone in it likes him and thinks he is still desirable. So, he isn't so much cheating *on* you as he is cheating *because* of you. Coming out of this zone involves trying to be as loving as you can. Take every opportunity to touch him. Hold him at night, and always give him that good morning kiss. It is as simple as this: to keep a lover faithful, be faithful in your love.

Meanwhile, don't turn him off by making selfish demands for specific sexual performances. Do you want to do some things that he doesn't like or cannot do, or have unusual preferences that he cannot or does not want to gratify because they go against his grain morally or hurt him emotionally or physically? Also, do you want it more frequently than he finds it desirable or even humanly possible to do because you confuse good sex with gorging yourself? Control your appetite all the better to satisfy his. Forcing him to do something that will hurt his feelings or his body is likely to drive him into the arms of someone more caring, someone who better satisfies his emotional needs by respecting his emotional and physical limitations more. Naturally, while you are doing these things, don't go to the opposite extreme and become excessively and rigidly uptight to the point that there is no passion left.

Of course, if nothing else works, and if you have the personality for it, you can always ignore his cheating. Many gay men do that. They simply decide to accept a new level of relationship. If this is you, you buy into the proposition that a half-baked relationship is better than none, forgive him when he cheats, and make up your mind just to ignore and go along with it. Think of it this way: the cells in his body change over every seven years, so even if you cannot forgive him now, if he stops this very day he will be a new person in less than a decade and you will have a new man on your hands who no longer requires your forgiveness; and that while he may have sex with an army that doesn't mean that he doesn't love and will not always come back to his private.

Polygamy

Polygamy differs from cheating in that it involves an arrangement where both of you are if not on the same page then at least in the same book. You both agree to have more than one partner and on the rules, if any, that cover what you may and may not do with the other men in your life. Here are some examples of such rules: one night of extramarital sex is okay, but I draw the line at two or more with the same man; outside sex is okay but not on weekends or holidays when the two of us should always be together; outside sex is okay as long as it goes no further than mutual masturbation; bigamy is acceptable as long as it is a four-square stable arrangement—no cheating allowed with extras; outside sex is to be limited to threesomes, that is, we will do what the decorators recommend and bring the outside in—for a treat for the night, a ménagerie a trois, or a stable stable. These rules work when they are put into place to maintain a clear distinction between permanent and temporary. They don't work nearly so well as guilt-reducers put into place to enable you to take back what you feel you did wrong—cleansing rituals that make Lady Macbeth's hand-washing look like a mere spot check. With or without limitations, arrangements can work when both parties find them acceptable. They don't, however, work when one person wants them and the other partner resentfully goes along, saying yes to something he actually objects to just to keep the peace and avoid a divorce. Partners who object but go along anyway because they will do anything to please their guy only feel hurt, unloved, rejected, and abandoned, and that will out. After quietly seething in a jealous rage they start a fight, stop caring about their relationship, or even become suicidal or depressed because they no longer care about anything at all.

Sandy and Bruce had an arrangement that didn't work for them. They had consciously and deliberately decided not to make sexual exclusivity an essential aspect of their relationship and so not to define their love and commitment sexually but instead to define it emotionally and spiritually. They felt that that way they could gratify their basic instincts, and maintain their identity both as gay men and as married gay men. They fooled themselves into believing that they were completely relaxed about what went on in their relationship. But they only *thought* they were in what they believed to be a comfortable "anything goes" zone where they had no serious scruples about sexual diversity. They only *felt* convinced that they wanted and liked the freedom to roam. That's because underneath there was always the fear that one would get a disease and pass it on to the other. They were also tortured by uncertainty as to where they stood with each other, and by the constant worry that their marriage would fall victim to the competition should one or the other meet someone new.

Besides, they dimly perceived how selfish they were being by ignoring the effects of their behavior on their guy—how they were seeking gratification for themselves regardless of the impact it was having on their partner. As a result, their supposed exciting journey was encumbered by a heavy satchel of hurt feelings, personal guilt, and fear of recrimination, retribution, and retaliation—a harsh burden to bear while traversing what was supposed to be a road that led only to happiness.

If you want to be monogamous but nevertheless find yourself being polygamous, start with **step one** and read my list of the disadvantages of polygamy. Here is a compendium of the disadvantages of an open, polygamous relationship. I am not being judgmental, just practical and realistic based on what I have learned from my own past relationships, from my friends, and from my work with gay couples.

An open relationship is never entirely relaxing. There is always a lot of intrigue, and you always have to worry about your lover being whisked away by someone new about to become the White Knight of his Days.

That of course can happen even when both partners are being faithful, but it happens more often when one or both of you are out there looking for someone new and different. Threesomes are especially dangerous. Straying together is particularly incompatible with staying together.

Polygamy leaves the true nature of your relationship in question. Neither of you knows exactly where you stand, where your relationship is going, or what your and its identity may be. Are you roommates, sex buddies, or husbands? Most likely, you are all three, which makes it most unlikely that you are doing any one thing absolutely right.

Polygamous partners rarely provide each other with sufficient companionship. They aren't there when you want them, and you have to spend many, many days, nights, and weekends alone while they are out there beating the bushes for bird.

An open relationship can be disrespectful and inconsiderate of his feelings. Polygamy is likely to leave him feeling bruised. Even if he is running around on you he may not want you running around on him. Even if he rejects you by running around with other men he will feel rejected by you if you do the same thing back to him. He just might say that your running around is okay because he thinks, "There is nothing I can do about it," or he thinks, "I am the problem; I am giving him too tight a leash," and "If I protest he will feel controlled and that will only make things worse," or because someone told him to let you go and if you come back to him he will know for sure that he is yours, or because you and all your friends share a good laugh if he even mentions the "M" word. But if you are off having outside sex, don't be surprised if he becomes unexpectedly temperamental, cops an attitude, then quietly forgets your anniversary or broods and flies off the handle about something else, like your not cleaning up the bathroom. And things can only get worse from here on, because the more humiliated and angry he feels the less sexy he will look and be—just like a peacock, which never looks quite as alluring after its crest has fallen.

Polygamy can be a great way to screw—yourself, when after years of running around you want to come back to him alone, perhaps because you are no longer so sexually desirable to other men. That can work, or it can be too late either because he won't forgive you completely, or at all, or because he has gotten involved with someone else. Just when your collagen is falling the fastest he may not be there to pick it up.

So look into the possibility that what you are doing is not the product of a preference but of a compulsion. It's a compulsion if it's not a true desire but a form of acting out. To find out, start by answering a simple question honestly: do the two of you not get along because you are polygamous, or are the two of you polygamous because you do not get along? Perhaps you two aren't as close as you might and should be, not because your gay hormones rage, forcing you to act like a feral cat, so that you must leave home and will just as soon as they open up the door and let you out, but because you have a serious relationship problem. So are you having a bad relationship because your sex is bad, or is your sex bad because you are having a bad relationship?

Step two involves using your new enlightenment to make the appropriate repairs. If you are acting out compulsively, deal with your sexual problems indirectly by dealing with any relationship problems you might be having directly. Relationship problems won't yield to attempts to revive and sustain sex by using artificial means like feathers, whipped cream, vibrators, or even the latest in designer pharmacotherapy. What you need to do is to work out any interpersonal difficulties that might be making for difficulties with frequency and performance, following the guidelines in this book.

Step three involves taking the cure before first thoroughly understanding the "disease." There is, after all, nothing that says you can't just stop scratching your itch without first finding out what is causing it. Every time he was tempted to wander, Alan forced himself to stop. He did that by remembering how easy it is when married to recall only the good things about being single and to forget the bad. He forced himself to stop recalling only those times of triumph when he melted into that new wonder he felt so proud of getting, and started recalling what it was like being one of those desperados out on the streets at four in the morning, and those times of despair when the new man he was so excited about didn't call him as promised or made a specific date with him then stood him up.

You can help set limits on and control both your fantasy life and your behavior by forcing yourself to have no-holds-barred sex with him and him alone, and all the time. I have seen many situations where frequency and exclusivity is enough to wear out and cut though sexual block. At the very least, this method might help you interrupt vicious cycling where bad sex produces worse sex until you panic, give up, and try someone new just because you are experiencing a mounting sense of desperation with your someone old.

Out of the Zones and into Monogamy

To me the advantages of monogamy are far greater than the (undeniable) sacrifices involved.

As should be absolutely clear by now, to my way of thinking monogamy, and the conviction, closeness, commitment, comfort, and convenience that go along with it, is the best, and basically the only truly workable, gay marital arrangement. Marcel and Chet had a strictly monogamous relationship. As they saw it, the same rules of conduct applied to things sexual as applied in nonsexual matters. They believed that you should no more run around on your husband than you should cheat on your business partner. They didn't think that being monogamous disavowed what it meant to be gay and that by being faithful to each other they were being a traitor to some important Gay Cause. Also they didn't think that being monogamous meant being a sissy, as if monogamy made them into that silly woman of song who resolutely stands by her man, and brags about it yet, not like her "more desirable" opposite, the butch cavemen stereotype their friends all wanted them to be like, you know, the kind who drags someone by the hair back to the hut and violates them, grunting before, during, and after.

They felt that the only thing they were missing from their lives was feeling ashamed of themselves and guilty about their actions. Feeling that love and sex were two intimately connected parts of a delightful whole, and sincerely believing that marriage meant relating to the whole person, not to just a part of him, they equated true love with sexual exclusivity, and felt that putting true love back in sex made for both better love and greater sex. Yes, one or the other might sneak in a sideways glance at someone else, but the unspoken rule was: don't undress him with your eyes. If you do look, only sneak a peek, then look quickly away so that you squelch your strong feelings about other men before the feelings, and you, run wild.

As you have probably guessed by now, to my way of thinking monogamy has to be absolute, because, like pregnancy, it is an all-or-nothing kind of thing. Absolute monogamy means no serious flirting. Serious flirting is divided attention and divided attention can be that single step that starts a journey of a thousand miles—away from home. Yes, your eyes might briefly wander, but your mind stays focused. Most partners are already worried enough about being cheated on. Flirting can only make them worry even more. Besides, if you are flirting, you are giving him the okay to flirt too, and where does that end? He will think, "Okay, you've taken the first step, so now I'll take the second," or, "You started us down this road, I'm going to complete the journey," and have that first affair that opens the door the crack that lets all those demons inside.

I sincerely believe that many of the gay men I have known personally or have seen in therapy are highly sensitive, highly attuned people. To them it doesn't make any real difference that your heart still belongs to daddy if you are seriously toying with sharing the rest of you. Flirting keeps you from becoming that desirable hot lover so supersaturated with amore that you crystallize out with the slightest shake. A really dark side of flirting is that it keeps you from concentrating and channeling all your sexual feelings toward him and him alone—from directing all your energy to him and giving him all you've got. So, my advice is to channel all your feelings to him and see if as a result you are a lot less tempted to drift off. When I was a kid I had an erector set and played with and adored it for years and years partly because it was one of the few toys I had. Today my niece has hundreds of toys she opens up and throws in the closet after fondling each one of them cursorily. You too can discover the lasting satisfaction of exclusive love whose depth and focus makes up for what it is missing in the thrills and the wonders of discovering new toys department. As an extra bonus you will discover what I learned several decades ago: monogamy is the world's greatest and truest erector set.

So stop looking around seductively at others and instead start looking at him exclusively. Hook your arm into his each time there is someone interesting and interested around as your way of sending him the message that you don't care about others because you love him both best and always. If he is the one constantly giving a cute number the eye, ask him what he is looking at and has in mind. Be sure to ask him a few times—a good way to tell him to stop without actually telling him off. If that doesn't work, then you just might have to have one of the dreaded sit-down discussions that you should avoid whenever possible, but not now.

Of course, you should not overdo prohibitions about flirting. You have to be careful not to make too much noise over what is essentially silence. You cannot be too sensitive. It is possible to expect too much because you want it all, or because you are too rigidly perfectionistic, making harsh rules that nobody can follow. You can't tell him that he cannot look at another man even if he is only trying to avoid bumping into him. You can't complain about his looking up from his restaurant meal to see if a star is at the next table. You can't expect to be in absolute control at all times, especially when your need for control is the product of your panicking about the possibility that he might leave you when in fact he has given you no real cause for alarm.

Here is a compendium of the main rewards of monogamy, shamelessly presented as my attempt to convince you that monogamy is the greatest gift you will ever have to give to each other.

Being monogamous is highly pleasurable. Yes, you have to make some tradeoffs and suffer a degree of deprivation, but that represents a good value. For with monogamy you give up something worthwhile, like sexual variety, to get something even worthier, like a trouble-free life. Monogamous men get not less but more and greater sexual pleasure by getting it steady from a steady. The sex is guilt-, hassle-, and disease-free, for the safer you are the less inhibited you feel. You can even think of monogamy as selfish because you are giving up so little yet in return you are getting so much. Also, you can love someone better when he is completely and irrevocably yours. Additionally, the sex actually becomes much more erotic as it becomes more focused and laser-like. Yes, monogamous sex changes over time, but it doesn't become less sexy, it becomes a different kind of sexy—not as intense, but more meaningful, making it paradoxically wilder at the same time that it gets tamer. Without release in cheating or polygamy, pressure and desire build between events leading to a much more explosive end result. Remember how gratifying it was to get something like food, water, and money after you were desperate to have it but couldn't get it for a long, long time? That is also true of sex. It's so obvious; still so many married people dissipate a little bit of their sexual energy here and a little bit there, in fantasy, and, unfortunately, in reality too, until sooner or later there is, in fact, very little left over for back home. The rules about sex are no different from the rules about the rest of life. Whether it's sex or soup, diluting it defies the common sense premise that what is worth doing is worth doing right, and all the way.

Monogamy conditions you to be monogamous, if only because inertia makes people keep doing today what they have been doing yesterday. With sex, as with everything else, practice makes perfect.

Monogamy is romantic. Think of Cinderella cheating on her prince. Those two kids really loved each other when they first met. Did they start running around on each other behind each other's back? We will never know for sure, but I don't think it likely. Why should your romance be anything less? Am I being too idealistic, and if so is there anything wrong with that? Why wouldn't you like to make you and your husband the model for the next fairy tale for time immemorial?

You ask what happens to sex when you and/or your lover get older and become less physically attractive. If you are the older partner you might begin to think, "How can he possibly still love me?" If you are the younger partner you might begin to yearn for someone younger, as you complain, "But his body is falling apart, wouldn't anyone feel turned off by that?" While getting older does present certain physical problems, in the main it presents emotional problems, and those can almost always be solved. If you are the older partner, you have to stop selling yourself short by thinking of yourself as undesirable. If you are the younger partner, you need to remember that disgust is an emotional state, so that his getting older is mainly a bitch when you are. While your true love for him doesn't make him any less wrinkled, it does make it less likely that you will be bothered by what wrinkles he has. For one thing, you will come to see each wrinkle as a permanent marker—not as a fatal flaw, but as badge of long-term togetherness, so that you will begin to count every wrinkle as a blessing that tells you that you are one of those gay men who has been favored enough to have had friend, lover, and companion for a lifetime.

Of course, let's face it, age differences can, going beyond the strictly emotional, create real difficulties too. The older man can only compensate up to a point for the changes that come with age with nice clothes, good grooming, and time at the gym, while the younger man's delight in having someone experienced and faithful can only improve the physical side of things so much. You have to actually do something about the sex. If you are the younger man and your older partner's aging begins to bother you, try having sex in a way that makes it unnecessary for you to actually face each other. Stick your head deep into him so that your view is blocked from the top and side giving you the effect of having blinders on, so that what you see will look pretty much the same as it always did. Or just shut your eyes and remember him as he once was—not as someone new, but as him as he was back then. That's the only way it is okay to fantasize having sex with "someone else."

What happens to sexual attraction when certain medical conditions make it difficult for you to have sex? Hal just got married, at age seventy-five, to a much younger man, Bill. Shortly after the marriage Bill became paralyzed and wound up in a wheelchair. Hal didn't mind, he just found new creative ways to enjoy the sexual experience, which I don't have to spell out for you. Many medical conditions, overt to subtle, can diminish sexual interest and performance capability. The specifics here are beyond the scope of my book. Also beyond the scope of my book are the complex issues associated with one or both partners being HIV-positive.

What's important is not to do what some people do and become impotent or just give up sex entirely because they feel guilty about exploring certain options.

7

Danger Zone 3: Dealing with Anger

It makes sense: a great relationship is a restful one, without outbursts of anger to disturb the peace. Conversely, there is nothing like anger to destroy one's rest, and unfortunately the relationship it destroys along with one's rest is almost always worth more than the issue that prompted the anger in the first place. So, the best idea is to avoid getting angry for starters, but, if you can't do that, to at least express your anger in a benign, civilized way. You can accomplish both these tasks by spotting when you are getting angry; understanding why you are getting angry and what you are getting angry about; identifying how you habitually express your anger (your "anger style," which I go on to define below); and channeling any anger you do express into a safe mode in order to minimize hurting his feelings and harming your relationship.

In the realm of anger styles, all of us get angry for more or less the same reasons. The big four are: you don't love me; you criticize me; you try to control me; and you think you are better than I am. But each of us expresses our anger differently: our individual anger style. Anger issues don't determine anger styles. These are determined not by the *content* of the anger but by its *mode of expression.* All anger styles seriously damage a marriage when done to excess. Only each does so in a somewhat different way.

There are three main anger styles: the abusive; the passive-aggressive, which consists of covert, subtle, provocative button-pushing; and the sadomasochistic, which consists of hurting him and needing and wanting to be hurt by him—usually both, but sometimes mainly one or the other. The three checklists that follow can help you determine if one, two, or all three anger styles are yours, and if they are yours if you are apt to go into one of the anger zones related to these anger styles.

Danger Zone 3a: The abusive anger style

This is your anger style if three or more of the following strongly apply to you.

- I often feel as if I hate him more than I love him.
- I am a real bitch, particularly, but not only, to him.
- Whenever I am cooking and he comes around, I feel like sticking a kitchen knife into him, and I can just barely keep myself from doing it.
- We fight all the time.
- Usually it's me who starts the fights.
- When we fight, I feel that I am always right and that he is always wrong.
- When we fight, I get very personal and call him names.
- He deserves to be yelled at and even hit because he pisses me off.
- I conclude that he done me wrong after selectively forgetting all the things that he ever did to do me right.
- I tend to be a vengeful individual. Getting back and getting even are more important to me than getting along.
- I have a long memory, and when I get mad I throw things from years ago up in his face.
- I get especially riled up when I feel he is rejecting me, criticizing me, controlling me, or competing with me—like when he tells me that he thinks that he is better than I am.
- I often call for a discussion about something that is bothering me, but

when we have it I don't talk about what is wrong and what needs to be done to fix it, but instead harp on how he screwed up, how he failed me in every possible way, and what he needs to do to make repairs.

- I love chaos, so just when things appear to be calming down I start them up all over again, and if he tries to get away from me I do what I can to close off his escape route.
- I sometimes storm out and go drinking, to a gay bookstore's back room, to the baths, or back to an old lover.
- I often threaten to leave him for good.
- I abuse him much the same way and for the same reasons my father or mother abused me.
- After I get angry, I feel terribly guilty about not having controlled myself.
- Guilt about my anger doesn't stop me from getting angry again, often the same way, and about the same thing, the next time.

Abusive partners express their anger directly. Typically, their anger outbursts start early in a relationship, and sometimes even on the honeymoon. Such guys become emotionally and sometimes even physically hurtful, blowing up and having temper tantrums that reduce their partners to tears and can do some real emotional or physical mischief. When they get angry, everything inside comes spilling out. Sometimes there is a point to their anger. At other times they are entirely off-base. They are certainly off-base when they rage that their guy is too sloppy when the real problem is that they are too neat and clean; that he is too whiny when the real problem is that they are upsetting him; that he is too competitive when the real problem is that they must always be the one on top; that he disagrees with everything they say and puts them down when the real problem is that they are wrong and out of line; that he is not sensitive enough to their needs when the real problem is that they are too needy; that he is too selfish when the real problem is that they are too self-absorbed; that his criticism is savaging and destructive when the real problem is that they fail to see how it is meant to be constructive and helpful; and that he is looking at them funny when they are in fact just ashamed of themselves about something they thought but didn't say, or something they did say, or do, that they anticipate, without evidence, that he might not like.

Hal was off-base when he yelled at Greg for being late with the cat's medication when in fact the problem was that Hal was so impatient that he couldn't even wait until Greg could get the tablet to dissolve in the cat's food. He was also off-base when he yelled at Greg for keeping him awake at night with his snoring when the real problem was that Hal was an insomniac who slept so lightly that Greg couldn't even breathe in and out without waking Hal up.

After getting angry, abusive partners often feel guilty, but the guilt has little or no effect on their subsequent behavior. Mostly instead of changing and doing better they make excuses for what they did. They often excuse their getting angry by citing the transcendental importance of being honest about how they feel and the health-giving benefits of getting their anger out of their system. They congratulate themselves for improving their mental state while forgetting the effect that their outbursts have on their partner's state of mind and on the state of their relationship. Yes, it is true that it is okay for you to feel and get a *little* angry. It is true that some *mild* aggravation can be a sign that your relationship is working, for it means that the two of you are related enough to get on each other's nerves. So, instead of being troubled about feeling *a bit* angry and feeling under pressure to make *all* your anger go away, you might just say to yourself, "Good, look how well we are doing" and let it go at that.

But don't go too far with this. While feeling a *little* anger is okay and even inevitable, and is even a creative first step in labeling problems on the way to finding friendly solutions, feeling too much and expressing more than a little anger, especially in a hurtful manner, can be fatal to your relationship. Sometimes one negative remark is never forgotten or forgiven. Little attacks accumulate and add up to turn him off and away from you, sometimes permanently. So, when it comes to getting angry, honesty is not necessarily the best policy, and the truth can set you free, but in the worst possible way.

Danger Zone 3b: The Passive-Aggressive anger style

This is your anger style if two or more of the following strongly apply to you.

- I get angry a lot but I do not express my anger honestly or openly.
- Instead of saying exactly what I mean and saying it directly, I express what I am thinking and how I feel indirectly, in roundabout ways, such as by becoming annoying, for example by having long debates on imponderables and other things that are short on importance, like "Should we dress a salad before serving it, or should we let the guests dress their own after they have put it on their plate?"
- I provoke him to get angry with me so that I can then get angry with him, making my anger at him look not like first but like second strike.
- I love to schedule big discussions sometimes for days in advance to talk about what is wrong, making him wonder for a good long time what exactly is up.
- I don't actually criticize him. I just never say anything nice to or about him.
- I play the blame game with physical symptoms, so that I tell him that I am pissed off in body language, having a pain in the anterior as my way to tell him that he gives me a pain in the posterior.

If you are a guy in the 3b anger zone, you are gentler than guys in the 3a anger zone, but you can be even more annoying, and the results of your anger even more devastating. That's because instead of having a temper tantrum and clearing the air, you keep at it, eventually completely fouling the atmosphere.

As a passive-aggressive partner you are always pissed about something or other. Typically you get even pissier first thing in the morning when you have just gotten up; when you are hungry; and when you first walk in the door after work, when you might say something like, "Don't talk to me for half an hour until I take off my shoes off, relax, and pour myself a drink."

When in the passive-aggressive zone you can neither shut your pissiness up inside completely nor express it openly, directly, and honestly. You don't have temper tantrums, you aren't physically abusive, and you don't get a reputation with him or with anyone else for being a nasty guy. Instead you express your anger indirectly and covertly, hitting on your partner in a way that leaves him not knowing for sure that he has actually been slammed. There are various possible scenarios here, like: refusing to budge when he wants something he ought to have and withholding it instead; preaching at him and being judgmental; killing him with kindness; asking loaded questions that hide accusations like, "You don't happen to know who broke this plate, do you?"; doing spiteful things like coming late to an event that is important for him; bumbling and making mistakes that drive him crazy; or just going out of your way to avoid doing something nice, as when you never criticize him, you only just never compliment him. In short, you push his buttons, goading him and keeping at it until he gets pissy with you. You start up with him, deny you did it, then blame him for having started the whole thing. Now you have the excuse you were always looking for to beat up on him even more, guilt-free, because, as you see it, he isn't your victim, you are his.

For years Mitch had wanted to get a new set of dining room chairs, but his lover George wouldn't let him because he thought that the old ones were just fine, even though the stuffing was coming out. As George said, "Who cares about that? You come to dinner to eat, not to sit on, my stuffing." George would also use positive gestures as vehicles for expressing negative feelings. For example, George felt Mitch was a slob who didn't clean up after himself when he did the cooking. But instead of saying how he felt, he would just walk around like an avenging vacuum straightening up after the normal cooking mess. Once George sent Mitch a Christmas card that detailed some of the problems they were having in their marriage. As George later smirked, "Boy you should have seen the look on his face when he opened that one up, and on December 25th yet." Or he would tell Mitch that he was going to leave for the weekend "so that you can have a rest from me for a while." When George wanted something he tortured Mitch by demanding it over and over again until he got his way as Mitch gave in just to avoid hearing George repeat himself one more time.

Characteristically, George would give Mitch a hard time over some abstract issue of minimal actual significance. In a revealing interaction of this sort, the cat was feeling sick and staring into space. Mitch said he thought that the cat looked "disoriented." He hadn't really arrived at this conclusion after doing a CAT scan. He was just making a passing comment. George, however, felt that he had to make it absolutely clear to Mitch that though the cat was indeed "obtunded" she didn't meet the formal criteria for being "disoriented." After years of all this, Mitch began cheating on George less because he wanted the sex and more because he just wanted someone to give him a little understanding, sympathy, and support.

Alf brought junk food home when his lover Marlon was on a strict diet for serious medical reasons, then left it around where Marlon could see and smell it, making it hard to resist. Alf's response to Marlon's suggestion that "If you must eat that stuff, eat it at the office" was to dismiss it with a curt "After all, you know, I'm not exactly forcing the food down your throat." Alf also found out precisely what Marlon disliked so that he could do that exactly. When Marlon put something here, Alf moved it there. Marlon liked the mat off the doorsill of their apartment. Alf knew this and put the mat back on the doorsill after Marlon pushed it off. Then when Marlon got agitated, Alf would make things worse by saying, "You are just too fussy for your own good" or "Why do you always have to be the one who gets his way?"

Carl and Frank adopted a son, Ben, of whom they were very proud. During the holidays Carl's workplace had a Christmas tree lighting ceremony. The night before the ceremony Carl told Frank that he wanted to take Ben to the tree-lighting and would pick Ben and Frank up at home (where Frank, having taken the day off, was babysitting their son). But when Carl arrived, he discovered that Frank and Ben were gone. Here's what had happened. As Carl had left work to pick Frank and Ben up, Frank had, on his own, decided to do Carl a favor and bring Ben to work so that Carl didn't have to make the long trip home to get them. Frank, at first sensing that there might be confusion, thought to pick up the cell phone and tell Carl that he was on his way and not to bother coming home to get them, but at the last minute he decided not to—as we later discovered, because he was mad at Carl for trying to hog Ben when Frank wanted Ben all to himself.

As a result of all the confusion, no one went to the tree lighting ceremony. Instead both men and the kid were wandering around for more than an hour looking for each other. This wasn't the first time Frank had pulled a trick like that, but still Carl was pretty unforgiving. For after the tree-lighting, which they missed, Carl walked around the office telling everyone what an idiot Frank was, and how he wished he had married someone else. This got back to Frank, who was deeply hurt and insulted by Carl's attitude and remarks. In response Frank gave Carl the silent treatment. In response to that, Carl started drinking then decided to go through with a little tree lighting he had been toying with all along—having an affair with someone hot he had had his eye on but had so far resisted plugging in.

Harold and Sam adopted a little girl. Harold loved her so much that each day when he came home he brought her a small gift. What was Sam's response to this largesse? To grouse that it was impossible to find anything to get her for Christmas because Harold brought her so much stuff every day of the year, all year round.

John's passive-aggressiveness took the form of sins of omission. John would never take his partner Burt to meet his family, or even mention him to them at all. His excuse was that he didn't want to hurt his family by telling them that he was gay. He did this though he knew that, especially on the major holidays, he was hurting Burt pretty badly by leaving him home alone to fend for himself. Burt couldn't bring himself to complain. He rationalized his reluctance to speak up with the thought, "Well, maybe I am being too demanding; after all, his family is from the old school, and people like that don't understand being gay." But still Burt's anger and disappointment just built and built until one day Burt started screaming that John didn't love him, adding that he had decided to leave him. Everyone blamed Burt for being a stupid romantic and said how lucky he was to have John even though John wasn't perfect. No one bought into Burt's sensible idea that he was right to complain that he ought to be a member of the family, not an object hidden away like a black sheep.

Once I had a lover, Bill, who took a sensitive tender moment to announce, with "perfect" timing, that he was going to see his ex-lover that evening, "just" for a social engagement. Not knowing what hit me, or knowing what hit me but feeling that I should be more accepting, and not so jealous, I started brooding, then drinking, trying unsuccessfully to put a lid on my feelings, only to ultimately lose complete control of myself, blow up, and "start" a fight. Of course, to those who came in in the middle of the story, and didn't know that Bill was playing me exactly the way he wanted—demolishing me slowly with effective button-pushing consisting of a slight provocation that others didn't notice because the provocation was too small to be apparent to the naked eyes of those who weren't personally involved and didn't really care that much—I looked like the evil genie. Then to a person they blamed not Bill for provoking me but me for being difficult. They said that I was imagining being provoked and overreacting to nothing. To a man, everyone said that I was viewing as negative the positive behavior of a lover who only wanted the best for me and tried and tried but could never seem to please me. That of course was the gem part of Bill's passive-aggressive plan—to quietly get my goat, so that I acted like a bad guy who was overreacting, when in fact I was an okay guy reacting appropriately to a provocation that was virtually invisible because the blows were being dealt so cleverly, subtly, and effectively that they could be easily passed off as "the normal annoyances of everyday life you should learn to put up with."

Now that I think back about that incident, I am reminded of something that happened to me recently at an upscale store. A woman cursed at me for breaking into the line when I was merely following the directions of the person in charge who had asked me back for some unfinished business. I told the woman who accused me of breaking into the line to watch what she said. She blew up at me and everyone took her side. Her provocation of me went completely unnoticed or was quickly forgotten, and the store personnel asked *me* to leave. In relationships, too, people regularly side with the passive-aggressive abuser, blame the victim for overreacting, turn the victim into a pariah who responds by drinking or cheating, and make him out to be the bad guy because he is the one to call for a divorce.

Some gay partners are so passive-aggressive that they even provoke physical abuse. I once had a patient, a man in his forties named Charles, who hit his young lover Milton on the head, and Milton reported him to an organization that protects gay youth from violence. What Milton forgot to tell the organization was that Charles also needed protection from Milton, because Milton's behavior was enough to piss off the Pope. He was a rebellious stubborn temperamental man who, to ice the cake, cheated on Charles. That didn't excuse Charles for becoming violent and hitting. It did, however, help explain why he acted that way, and point to a remedy better than bringing in reinforcements and heading for divorce court.

Here are some special passive-aggressive don'ts, things to avoid doing in order to avoid destabilizing your relationship by making your guy chronically uncomfortable and unhappy.

Don't tease him. Nat kept offering to buy his lover Hal a piano so that he could practice at home, only to balk at the last minute because he thought it too expensive and because pianos were, according to him, instruments of pleasure, not good long-term investments.

Don't turn a straightforward request, for example to straighten up the house, *into a personal criticism*—such as "You are a dirty person."

Try not to catastrophize, so that if he is a *bit* sloppy you respond by telling him that if he doesn't stop he is going to drive you *absolutely* crazy.

Never double bind him, so that you demand to be free when you feel dominated, demand to be dominated when you feel free, and complain that he never gives you what you want or that he always does the opposite of what you ask him to do. Here's an example of a double-bind courtesy of a patient's mother-in-law. She asks him for advice, if he doesn't respond demands to hear his take on things, and if he does respond complains that he is telling her what to do, and says she doesn't take marching orders from anyone, him included, or especially. Ed asked Harris to tell him what was wrong. He said, "Express your feelings honestly so that I can know how to make you feel better." Then after Harris said what was on his mind, Ed slammed into him because he didn't like what he heard. So Harris vowed to shut up in the future. Only now Ed complained that Harris wasn't sufficiently interested in him to pay attention and answer him when he asked him a question, and wasn't honest enough to speak up about what he was thinking and tell him what was bothering him.

Never bad-mouth him behind his back, especially to a third party who is just panting to have a hand in ruining your relationship. Here is an example of what Sal said to Howard behind hubby Jan's back: "Never be married to the same man for forty-one years. Now that that my old fart husband Jan has broken his hip, I cannot keep my massage appointment with Bruno who is rumored to be the best masseuse in L.A. I wanted to find out if Bruno was as cute as he was good. Our mutual friend Paul told me how great a masseuse he was, but not what he looked like." Statements like that are guaranteed to get back, and to hurt. Even saying something as totally mild as "he is difficult to live with" could bounce back elaborated as a serious complaint. Next your guy will feel betrayed and try to make himself whole by finding another partner. So don't ever forget: if you must talk out of school, say only positive things. That way either only good things can get back or, if a third party lies about what you said, you will at least be able to defend yourself because you will remember what you actually did say.

Don't do anything to deliberately arouse his suspicions. Don't take special care of your appearance or buy sexy underwear just to drive him wild with distrust, knowing that he won't be able to say anything about it for fear of looking pathologically jealous. If you have done something along these lines that you maybe shouldn't have, reassure him that you won't do it again, then act in a way that inspires him to believe you. Certainly never blow his mind by calling him paranoid when he has real reasons to be suspicious of you.

Never provoke him to hit you just so that you can have him exactly where you want him—cowed, regretful, guilty, afraid of physical and legal retribution, and willing to do almost anything just to be let off the hook and given another chance.

Stop hiding specific complaints about him as nonspecific but see-right-through-whining, as when you say, "I hate my life" as a way to tell him, "I am displeased with our relationship." I once whined until Bart, my old lover, agreed to leave a perfectly good apartment with two bedrooms and a nice view in the heart of Greenwich Village. Bart loved it there, but I said we had to move because they opened a pizza parlor across the street and I thought that a big red neon sign that read "Mamma Mia Whadda Pizza" was incompatible with my lofty self-image. So I made us move to The Pretending-to-be-the-Upper-East-Side, near Beekman Place, only I couldn't tolerate how snobbish it was, believing it was too lofty for my quintessentially modest self-image. So I made us move back to the West Village and, now, years later, with Bart long gone, Michael and I are living in a nice apartment with a view right across the street onto a bright red neon sign that reads: "Whadda Pizza, Mamma Mia." Bart finally correctly perceived that it wasn't the locale that was bothering me. He was perceptive enough to understand that what was bothering me was living in any place at all with him in it.

Don't give backhanded compliments, for example, saying, "You look better" in a way that implies, "You didn't look so good before."

Don't make comparative statements, so that the question arises, "Compared to what?" Instead of saying, "You are looking better today" say instead, "You look great," and leave it at that.

Stop demanding he take your side when you know he can't or won't, because he is right to disagree with you, then after backing him up against the wall, for the hundredth time in just the same way, and about the same, wrongheaded thing, telling him when he complains that, "If you loved me you would support me."

Never provoke him by doing exactly what you already know drives him crazy. Don't learn about his sensitive spots just so that you can poke him where he hurts. Don't rile him up by taking positions on religion or politics that you know he doesn't agree with then insisting that he see things your way. Matt, even though he knew that his partner Jerry was a very liberal, very permissive individual tolerant of differences, would nevertheless stereotype ethnic groups and make fun of transsexuals and drag queens every chance he got. If he is a neat freak, stop dropping your clothes on the floor and start picking up after yourself. If he is very dependent, stop threatening in a pique to leave him. If he is uncertain about being loved, stop telling him your fantasies about the delivery man who just passed and quit bringing home "romantic films" that send the message that the only way you can get it off with him is to get it on with someone else.

Never give him the silent treatment (or do any other form of hostile removal). Don't come home at night and hide out in your room, telling him you have to have some time alone and can't be bothered by him until you unwind, only to emerge an hour later saying, "Now I am ready for you," your way of telling him, "Coming home to you is so traumatic that I need a whole sixty minutes to get myself together." If you do that you may make him so desperate to please you that he will try anything to get a positive rise out of you, then if you don't respond start a fight just to get some sort of reaction out of you.

Do not fail to be sensitive and responsive to his needs. Don't be late coming home without even bothering to call. Don't go to bed before he does without that goodnight kiss. Don't seriously delay responding to a request to handle some pressing matter. If he asks you if you can do this or that, don't take a week to get back to him with your answer as your way to express having mixed feelings about doing anything at all for him.

Don't give him precisely what he doesn't want or something he does want precisely when he doesn't want or no longer wants it. Don't ask him what he wants for his birthday, and when he says "A shirt," get him a tie, or get him nothing then give him a shirt—two weeks later, along with a belated birthday card. Also don't ask for something not because you really want it but because you know that that is exactly what he would prefer not to give you.

Don't turn what he gets into what you lose. If he wears your clothes, don't complain, "I was going to wear that to the spaghetti dinner at the lodge tomorrow night but probably I won't be able to because you put stains on it like you put on everything you touch." Just remember that your clothes are his clothes too, and graciously lend him everything in your wardrobe, and if he puts a stain on some of your favorites, just take them to the cleaners, throw them in the wash, or toss them out.

Don't put him on an impossibly rigid schedule. Don't, as some gurus suggest, schedule discussions weeks in advance or, again as some gurus suggest, pencil in times into your busy schedule for lovemaking, just so that you can let him wait until it is time, and you are ready.

Never dig him sarcastically. Subtle putdowns can be the most devastating of all. That is because if the putdown is subtle, he cannot prove you put him down and instead will likely start beating himself up for being oversensitive. For example, don't ask him a question and then, after he answers it, immediately ask someone else the same question as if to say, "I don't respect your opinion all that much."

Never make jokes at his expense. Especially avoid jokes about infidelity. Don't look at a cute number and say, "I may be married but I am not dead yet" or "I can look as long as I don't touch, can't I?" then go on to laughingly tell him your private fantasies as if they are not to be taken seriously just because you qualify them with, "I might think it but I will never do it." Telling jokes like that is like making wisecracks about bombs at the airport. All lovers are very sensitive people. Even the ones who act like sluts and talk promiscuity can be easily hurt by such behavior on your part, but they won't tell you that because they are ashamed of the way they feel, so they try to act as if they are insensitive when they are in fact hurting badly inside.

You do not need to be completely, brutally, honest. Never say what exactly is on your mind when what you have to say is at all hurtful. Always ask yourself when you are tempted to think that honesty is the best policy: "Are you telling him the truth, or are you rubbing his nose in something?"

You must make a clean break from your past. Don't spite and insult him with nostalgia. Be especially careful to put your old lovers behind you. Certainly drop the "Nothing is the same now that Judy is dead" mentality. Sending the message that there is something better about a past without him in it than about the present with him around belittles him and makes him feel unappreciated, disrespected, unimportant, and unloved. Instead be clear: things are much better for me now that Judy is finally dead, and you are alive.

Do not make a list of what's wrong with him and the relationship then "accidentally" leave the list out where he can find it. Charles wrote his grievances out and left the composition in a place where his lover Connie was bound to run across it. Connie was very hurt and extremely insulted and life at home was never really the same again.

Always listen and act constructively and correctively when he has a point. If he is right on the money, buy into what he says and don't have defensive blaming knee-jerk reactions of the "It's not me, it's you" sort that keep you from hearing his important message, having it sink in, and responding accordingly. Here's an example of how not to behave from an incident in my life. I am allergic to sunflower seeds. The restaurant I was eating in served me a salad full of them. I ate it, then halfway through realized what I had done. I called the waitress over to ask her if these little things in the salad were indeed sunflower seeds. She said yes. I said that I was allergic to them. I was anticipating that she would help me call an ambulance. Instead she brought over the menu and told me to read it to see that they were listed and so the problem was not that I had eaten something dangerous but that I didn't scan the list of ingredients before chowing down. She was technically correct, and nothing happened to me from the seeds, but I don't want to tell you what tip I left her, and in relationships, that's the payoff, isn't it?

Don't promise him something then drag your feet about giving it to him. Especially don't offer to improve then do nothing to change.

Don't overplay hard to get in the belief that that game will make you wanted even more. I have found that it is much easier and better to win at playing hearts than at playing poker. So play "I'm all yours" where you throw yourself into his arms and on his mercy. Yes, people often want most what they cannot have, or do the opposite of what others expect them to do, so that acting nonchalant can be the best way to get others to give you what you really want. We are all a little bit paradoxical in our reactions. It's in our guts and maybe even in our genes. Still, playing hard to get is a ploy. Like other ploys it might work for today, but sooner or later playing hard to get makes you harder to want.

Stop playing the self-blame game. Can the repetitive self-deprecating "I'm so sorry" remarks. More than one apology begins to constitute an attack. Don't, for example, say, over and over again, "I am such a klutz" after you drop and break a dish when that is your way to accuse him of putting the dishes up so high that no one could ever get them without having an accident.

Don't be hypocritical. Don't pull the "Do what I say, not what I do" bit, or the "It's not okay when you do it, only when I do it" bit, or the "When it comes to me little things mean a lot, but when it comes to you a lot of things mean too much" bit.

Do take him seriously. Stop complaining that he is sweating the small stuff. Remember that if it's meaningful to him, even if it is small stuff to you, it is big stuff for him, period.

Stop blaming him for your own problems. For example, don't cover up your selfishness by complaining that he gives you a hard time whenever you want anything.

Let petty resentments go. Petty resentments that you carry into bed with you can easily destroy not only your sex life but also your whole relationship. Paradoxically, for some men closeness is their special time to start feeling resentful. At times of closeness, they are most tempted to hurt the one they love the most because they sense how needy and vulnerable he is, and know that's when they can have the maximal effect and get away with it.

Don't play the game of giving him enough rope to hang himself. Permissive partners express their aggressiveness indirectly by failing to set limits on their guy or by failing to set them high enough. They express their anger by allowing their relationship to deteriorate by refusing to stop their partner from destroying it. They lay traps for their partner, setting him up to fail. They don't tell him what they want, need, and expect just so that they can prove their point that they are being disdained and rejected, and right to bitch about it.

Danger Zone 3c. The sadomasochistic anger style

Guys in this zone express their anger by being hurtful to, and by fixing to be hurt by, a partner. *Nonsexual* sadomasochism involves hurting him emotionally, for example by calling him names, or by saying you hate him and have the urge to kill him; or hurting him physically, for example by hitting him. *Sexual* sadomasochism involves activities ranging from play biting or pleasurably delaying orgasm to inflicting or asking for physical abuse in the form of bondage with handcuffs, fisting, or drinking his urine.

Sadomasochistic partners believe that emotional or physical *pain* is desirable either for itself—as a feel-good sensation on its own—or because it makes a pleasurable substitute for something even more painful, so that a partner might gladly suffer the pain of being humiliated to avoid the pain of being abandoned and experience the pleasure of feeling safe. Or they feel that emotional and physical *pleasure* is inherently undesirable; for example, they believe that feeling good is amoral and that pain is conducive or even essential to moral superiority. So they make everything a struggle in the belief that it's wrong for good things to come too easily, meaning that they are only able to accept good times if they had a bad time getting there.

A degree of nonsexual and sexual sadomasochism, especially that associated with occasional submission or dominance, is not only compatible with, but can even be necessary for, a goodly amount of marital bliss. But too much can threaten a relationship or court physical danger. Particularly dangerous is the need to have a "masochistic triumph" along the lines of "See, I managed to prove once again that nobody gay can ever be happily married," so you break up with him just so that all your friends can feel sorry for you and hold you in their arms as they feel your pain and weep along with your sadness.

Here is a checklist to help you determine if yours is a sadomasochistic anger style. This is a very important checklist, because more than five positive responses might mean that not only your relationship but also your or his life is in actual and immediate danger.

- I see everything that happens in our relationship from the point of view of who is pure and who is foul.
- I sometimes want to hurt him and I sometimes want to be hurt by him.
- No equal partners for me. I like to be either dominant or submissive.
- I love pain and suffering.
- Suffering and making him suffer gives me a kind of sensual pleasure.
- I see pain and suffering as conducive or even essential to moral superiority.
- Suffering and making him suffer makes me feel real, and whole. For example, the best time I ever had in my life was when I scheduled myself and my ex-to-be into what he thought would be a lovely two-week vacation just so that I could tell him under the Tuscan sky on the first day of our trip that it was all over between us.
- I love to torture him by keeping him guessing as to exactly where he stands with me.
- I willingly undergo a lesser pain to avoid suffering another greater pain. For example, I will let him humiliate me all he wants if that will keep him from leaving me.
- I love to go back over my life and torture myself with all the bad things I did when I was young and to torture him with all the bad things that he did to me earlier in our relationship, and is still doing to me now.
- I love fights. Fighting gets all the anger out of me, I fall exhausted to

the ground, and I so love making up when it's all over that I can't wait to do it again.

- My mantra is "Fight, but don't fight fair, fight to win."
- I love to involve third parties in our fights. My favorite line is, "Look at what he did to me; what do you think of that?" I always tell my friends half the story so that I can get all their sympathy.
- I don't deserve anything good in life. I feel as if I am a bad person and that is why I feel I deserve to be hurt, punished, and abused.
- I don't mind his criticizing and punishing me. It feels good, like I'm back in parochial school.
- He needs to be criticized and punished at least a little. No one is perfect, and he in particular can use an occasional reminder of that, particularly when he is acting like he deserves it.
- I don't want my marriage to succeed; I want it to fail.
- Nobody can help me fix my relationship and the more they try the worse it gets. I am, and it is, destined to fail no matter what. Trying to help things get better only makes them get worse.
- I often fantasize about how my tearful, caring, concerned friends and worried family will sympathize with me because of all my suffering in this relationship.
- I often take out my unresolved rage from childhood hurts on him.
- Basically we are all sinners.
- Gay sex is a sin. God doesn't want us to put it where we do. That's why I prefer loving someone who doesn't want or really enjoy sex.

Here are some ways out of anger zoning. Clearly some of these correctives will be applicable to all, while others will be more helpful for one or the other, styles of anger.

Step one involves just calming down. You are about to boil over and blow up and you even feel like you are about to kill him. Instead, cool it, and avoid a fight. Here are some hints about how to do that:

Talk to yourself about the consequences of getting angry. Anticipate how guilty you will feel afterwards should you continue to piss him off, or blow up at him. Consider your specific life circumstances and if you can really afford to be a bitch. Donald and Bill were never apart except when Bill went to work. They did everything together including accompanying each other to professional meetings. Donald liked the relationship that way, partly because he tended to be rather possessive; partly because he tended to be rather prissy about sexuality in general; and partly because he always liked to be in control of any situation he was in, and certainly this one. But the closeness between them did expose him to problems if something happened either to the relationship (that was unlikely) or to Bill. Clearly Donald had to do everything that he could to avoid getting angry with Bill, for his own well-being, as well as the relationship's.

Try to sit on your anger until it passes. Do as I once did. A neighbor's dog was barking. I asked my neighbor what he was barking at and he said, "You." Why I asked? "Because he doesn't like you," he answered. This isn't worth getting all upset about, is it? As it turned out, he was just kidding. Yeah. So I said nothing. The dog still barks at me, but at least the neighbor still talks to me—when I don't have time to turn the corner before we run into each other. So follow my example and instead of saying something that you can never take back just wait until the impulse to say something mean, bitchy, or evil goes away. You won't be satisfied for the moment, but you might still be together for the ages.

Step two involves understanding your anger through and through. Whichever anger type you are, it almost always helps to discover exactly where it and you are coming from. Understanding your anger starts with distinguishing actually being provoked from only feeling that way. If you are actually being provoked, you have to deal with him. But if you just feel provoked, you only have to deal with yourself.

If you must discuss feeling angry with him, only talk with him about rational anger, that is, anger that is due to justified jealousy over his cheating, or justified annoyance about his stubbornly refusing some perfectly reasonable request you have made. Never talk about irrational anger, for example, the kind that is due to his loving you too much. Talking with him about your irrational anger is just plain wrong. If you must talk about your irrational anger, talk about it to your religious advisor or to your therapist.

Consider the possibility that if you feel provoked when he isn't provoking you, you may be displacing your anger from elsewhere onto him. For example, ask yourself if you are mistaking him for your boss, so that your boss pushes your buttons but you don't say anything to him and instead save it up for home and when you get there crap all over your guy when you first walk in the door. Or perhaps you are mistaking him for your parents, in effect "parentalizing" him. Take me. I hate to be teased in large measure because my father would promise me something then not deliver it for at least a year. So if you want to see me turn purple, offer to do something for me then drag your feet about actually doing it. Or, take Sol. When he was a child he had a crazy grandmother living with him, but each time he complained to his mother that his grandmother was driving him nuts his mother responded by taking the grandmother's side and criticizing Sol for complaining about her dear mother. Now if Sol's lover Fred even tries to say something Sol doesn't agree with but still needs to hear, Sol thinks Fred is against him just because he isn't with him, so he gets angry, and starts a fight.

Making your lover a substitute for a bad parent is obviously a bad idea. But even good parent substitutes might not satisfy. Partners who select good mother substitutes predictably get angry after they find that they fail them. They feel that they have failed them by not giving them the quality of mother love they originally got and also expect now, or by being so much like their real mother that it becomes impossible to have sex with them. Partners who select good father substitutes also predictably find that they fail them. They pick them to be strong like the father they never had, only to come to hate them should they not match up to their real father, or they pick them to be weak like the father they actually had all the better to compete with them, only to disdain and disrespect them for being the same sort of wimp that their father was.

Alternatively, if your anger is unprovoked maybe you are in one of the specific zones I describe in chapters 5–13. Maybe you are a *selfish* person who feels keen disappointment over not getting anything, big or small, that you want or need, ranging from a birthday remembrance to all his love for yourself; a *suspicious* person who has a great deal of difficulty trusting and flies into a rage after seeing sinister things in a partner's innocent behavior; a *control maven* who gets pissed off because you feel your husband is somehow pushing you around in ways ranging from messing with your schedule to messing with your life; a *control sponge*, so that instead of complaining "You always tell me what to do," you complain that "You never take over when I need you the most, leaving me feeling panicky and confused"; or a very *competitive* guy who hates losing out so that you have a rage reaction if he bests you in any way at all. As I have found over and over again, fear of commitment is a very common source of unprovoked anger. To anticipate my discussion of the fear of commitment zone in chapter 8, I have seen many gay men who become mean and nasty to and critical of their partners because, fearing the love they have inside of themselves, they deliberately, if unconsciously, angrily demean their partners to make them appear to be less lovable so that now they don't have to get so close to them.

You should suspect that your anger originates in one of these specific zones if you tend to suddenly and repeatedly become irrational over the same thing. To tell if this is the case, look for patterns; that is, permanently sore points of yours that lead you to feeling poked and prodded, though you are merely being gently stroked.

Of course, your anger can be both unprovoked and provoked, which just gives you two jobs to do. You have to understand where you are coming from so that you can come from someplace else, and you have to see clearly what he is actually doing to upset you and deal with what is wrong between the two of you.

Merv invited his whole family down for the holidays without first checking with Judah to see if that was okay. Bad thing to do, so Judah got annoyed, and understandably so. But while it's true that Merv provoked Judah, it's equally true that Judah was much too easily provoked because Judah, being too possessive of Merv, saw anyone, Merv's family included, as an interloper. And who is to say who is right in the following interpersonal skirmish: Vic complained that Fran pissed him off by adopting six street cats. Fran complained that Vic wasn't humanitarian enough. Vic complained that Fran was overdoing it with the humanitarianism. Then Fran complained that Vic was selfish and unfeeling not only about cats but also about humans and about one human in particular—Fran. It was a draw.

Step three involves expressing what anger you cannot master in a relationship-saving way. Suppose your anger won't quit and then breaks through and you find yourself getting angry in spite of yourself. You can still minimize the effects of your anger on him and on your relationship by doing some quick damage control. I have some suggestions:

Censor your anger as it spurts from your lips. Watch not only the content of what you say but also your timing and tone of voice. Soften what you say by turning your mind into the same sort of censoring device they use for live talk shows. Put a seven second delay between your thoughts and your words. Use the time to quickly stop, look, listen, and think, instantaneously cleaning up your act by changing what you are about to say into something more acceptable to hear.

Sublimate your anger. For example, try transforming it into something else, like pity, as you go from "I am angry with you," to "I feel sorry for you because you cannot help yourself." Or, go punch a punching bag instead of punching him in the face.

Just try changing the subject. Displace your anger from a highly-charged, personal topic to a neutral, impersonal topic. Get all in an uproar over a political issue instead of over something bad you feel your guy did to you. The president of the United States always makes a great lightning rod to drain your anger away from your husband. And as you by now may have guessed, some presidents serve that purpose better than others.

Try expressing angry thoughts detached from angry feelings. That is, say what you have in mind, but say it without passion. After deciding just what point you want to make, make it exactly, but coolly and with calculation. Talk softly. That makes it impossible to yell, and yelling only feeds on itself, revving you up so that you get angrier and angrier.

Don't get personal. Focus on the deed, not on the doer. Don't be like Ned, who wanted to tell Randy that he was mad at him for treating him as if he were invisible by inviting his parents over for dinner without first checking to see if that were okay. But instead of just saying what he thought and stopping there, Ned continued on, telling Randy that he felt that Randy was a selfish pig. As a result, he made Randy feel bad without ever actually making his point.

If in spite of it all, if you do lose control, at least apologize afterwards. You might not be able to take back what you said completely but you can at least minimize some of the bad effects of your temper tantrum after the fact.

Now, what if your man is the angry one?

If your husband is prone to this particular zone, **step one** involves making certain you aren't provoking him, and that means doing everything you can do to avoid pissing him off. There is enough suffering in this world that you cannot do anything about without creating some electively just for the sadistic pleasure you get from inflicting pain, or the masochistic pleasure you get from being victimized.

Step two involves showing some concern when he gets angry. Whether or not it is you who have made him angry, don't avoid him when he is in his angry zone. Instead recognize that he is hurting and soothe him. Instead of "Be back when you get over that" make it "Honey, let me rub your back until you feel better."

Step three involves not getting unduly upset just because he gets a tiny bit angry with you. Distinguish his being slightly annoyed with you from his being miffed, from his being angry, from his being furious, from his urge to kill, from his coming at you with a knife. Ignore mere passing clouds and only respond when he is stuck on something to the point that it actually blots out your sun. Always distinguish things he says in anger that are simply the product of a kind of temporary insanity on his part—as when he says something he doesn't really mean because he is momentarily bent out of shape and pissed—from his making a negative positional statement that reflects his being zoned out for a lifetime.

Step four involves trying just not to hear his anger. Try doing what people do when they live along a busy highway—they just don't hear the traffic anymore. Try not letting his passive-aggressiveness get a rise out of you. Do what we do with Michael's parents. They are always late. They regularly and fiendishly call to say they are just leaving when they should be arriving, then speak of the heavy traffic holding them up even though they have been down this route before and should have built the heavy traffic into their timing. We just get a good laugh out of it, and don't make it a bigger problem than it in fact is. Is he always a few moments late? Find something to do while you are waiting for him. Is he sloppy around the house? Pick up that mop and clean up that floor yourself. Instead of taking the bait, restructure the interaction by defining mutual goals and by asking him to work with you toward achieving them.

Step five involves trying to put as good a spin as possible on what he says and does. You won't get so upset about, or be so unforgiving of, his anger if you try to extract something reasonably positive from the negative, and some humaneness from the apparent inhumanity. If your guy invites his family over without first checking with you, perhaps he does that because he feels isolated from his family, or scared to death that you might not let him go through with his plans if you found out about them first. He bitches at you about the horrible pillows on the sofa? You should not say, "We will get new ones so that you don't *complain* anymore about them." Instead say, "We'll get new ones so that you don't *suffer* anymore."

Saul gave Manny a hard time whenever Manny tried to landscape the house. This bush was no good, that shrub was wrong, and as a result they wound up not landscaping anything and having a bare house and lawn. At first glance it seemed as if Saul were deliberately trying to piss Manny off. But further exploration revealed that Saul just had a neurotic thing about bushes and shrubs. He was afraid to brush against them because he thought that they harbored harmful and maybe even poisonous bugs. The resolution? They decided to have a sculpture garden, with just a few little trees in an out-of-the-way place, one you didn't have to go near if you didn't want to come into contact with them.

Taking all the blame on yourself is a useful method for handling desperate emergency situations, as when a fight is about to break out. If he gets irrationally exasperated and snaps at you, don't say, "I hate it when you do that" but instead say, "I was just trying to be helpful, but it looks like I made a mistake and just pushed your wrong button. Sorry." That doesn't mean walking around depressed all the time moaning about what a horror you are. It does, however, mean acknowledging and even overemphasizing anything you might have done to contribute to a bad situation and promising to improve the next time. In my opinion what temporary risk there is to your self-esteem from excessive self-blame is more than outbalanced by the self-enhancing qualities of having a great relationship for a lifetime.

Step eight involves injecting as much positivity as possible into your relationship in between episodes of anger zoning. A generally positive relationship can survive more anger than a generally negative one. If your life is a continuous party, you won't mind nearly so much if your angry zoned-out hubby crashes it every once in a while.

8

Danger Zone 4: Overcoming Fear of Closeness and Commitment

The following chapter is for those of you who are so afraid of commitment that you create marital difficulties with your partner just so that you don't have to get too close to or become too intimate with him. If you check off more than half the items in the following checklist, it may mean that you are one of those guys who actually get so anxious about your marriage's succeeding that you deliberately arrange to have it fail.

- I don't make any plans in advance because I feel trapped when I cannot get out of something, anything, even if it's only a dinner date.
- Marriage is an especially tight spot that makes me long for my space.
- I often think about how wonderful it would be to sit at home by myself surrounded by the things I love, like my valuable collection of lovely appliquéd teacups.
- I have been married before, and many times, but not for long, because all the while I was married I asked myself, "How am I going to get out of this should I want to?"
- I was always the one who left, and often without warning. More than one hubby came home to find me gone.
- It's great being gay because, at least if you don't sign a domestic partnership agreement, you can beat a path out of a relationship

whenever you want to and without a lot of stupid paperwork.

- No matter how great my sex life is with him, I still feel strongly attracted to the buzz of getting it on with someone new.

- I feel especially attracted to men who are unavailable for the long term, such as men who play hard to get or who are already married.

- I have completely lost interest in him sexually. He still wants it, but, after all, how many times can you do it with the same person?

- Marriage compromises my identity. It keeps me from being me and from being free.

- I don't get close to him so that I won't get so upset if he rejects me.

- I don't get close to him because I feel sheepish about and ashamed of my positive feelings. So it is easier for me to have an argument than a love fest.

- I choke on the words "I love you" and "You are the one for me" to the point that they never leave my mouth.

- I don't look to him for love. In fact, I hate it when he fawns all over me. It gives me the creeps because I feel that he is acting like a wimp.

- The way he is gives me plenty of reasons to cruise, cheat on, and leave him.

- We aren't really compatible. For example: he isn't as much in touch with his feelings as I am; he gets hysterical over nothing when I am the calm stoic type who thinks that sweating anything at all, even the big stuff, is a waste of time, and even a sin; and he loves boorish baseball when I love the much more sublime chamber music.

- I prefer independence to commitment. Marriage isn't right for everyone and it isn't right for me. As far as I am concerned, the single life is just as good and valid as the married life, and don't let anyone tell you otherwise.

- Screwing around is the essence of being gay.

These days in some segments of the gay community there is a lot of talk, pro and, sometimes it seems, mostly con, about committed monogamous relationships. If there is any big difference between the gay and the straight community, it is that fewer gays than straights openly condemn polygamy within a committed relationship. They see it as okay, or normal, not as a symptom of a fear of commitment. Indeed, some gay individuals condemn not polygamy but those who advocate monogamy. They say that people who advocate one marriage to one guy are on a mission to shake queer dudes out of their entrenched gay ways, and they condemn monogamy itself as uncool because it devalues what it means to be gay. Some are pretty open about how they feel. Say one word about the wonders of monogamy and you get shot down. I recently did a little poll. I asked ten gay men what they thought of a newspaper column written by a man previously vocal in print about being in a long-term committed relationship. The columnist had said, "On Sunday morning in a home improvement store, it just doesn't get better than picking out power tools in one aisle—and cruising 'em in the next one over." The result of my unscientific poll? Not one of the ten gay men I showed the column to even batted an eyelash.

Of course, there is a great deal of room for differing individual views about committed monogamous long-term relationships. What is important is to make certain your view, whatever it is, is an indication of your true preference, not of a compulsive need to think a certain way that reflects not your thoughts about what you really want out of your marriage but your terror about what your marriage might hold in store for you. You need to ask yourself "Do I really want to be polygamous or do I fear being monogamous?" and then, "If I fear being monogamous, is it because of what being monogamous means?" and, if that's the case, "What exactly might that be?

Carl complained that his lover Ben was stifling him by always being there for him when he needed him. Carl recalls that once or twice in the beginning of their relationship Ben came about half an hour late to an engagement, but after Carl made it clear that he would like him to be on time, Ben became punctual and even got a cell phone so that he could call Carl in case he was unavoidably delayed. However, proving that with men who fear commitment no good deed of intimacy goes unpunished, Carl, instead of thanking Ben for his care and concern, became annoyed at him because he saw him as a patsy, an excessively compliant pushover type of guy, *not* what Ben would have preferred, someone strong, not so malleable, someone to push *him* around, not the reverse.

Now all Carl could think about was how wonderful it would be to be single again, because being single would be better than being stuck with this loser who was trying just a little too hard to get what Carl called "disgustingly close and frighteningly intimate." Next, the rationalizations flew, all of them churned out by Carl's rearoused fear of getting close: "I hate: fighting about the remote control and the one bathroom we have; his waking me up in the middle of the night when he gets up to pee; his playing the TV too loud; his never picking his socks up off the floor; his putting wet towels on the bed; his not serving the dinner hot enough; his cooking with too much salt; his serving portions that are always either too big or too small; his keeping the car a mess and never washing it; and his insisting that we live within our means when we have all those credit cards just itching to be swiped." Next thing you know, Carl, wanting to be free, and "me," started cruising every night, leaving Ben sitting home alone feeling hurt, abandoned, and terrified about the future, so much so that Ben began to feel that he was not dealing with a fear of commitment, he was dealing with a commitment to be feared. So now it was Ben who made the decision to put a little distance between himself and Carl, and he decided to do that by starting an affairette of his own.

Step one out of your fear of commitment zone involves an attitudinal change. It may be true that because you are gay you can always leave when you want to go, but it's a much better idea first to make up your mind to stay and second to work things out so that you don't have to go anywhere. Decide once and for all that you will stop wanting to grow on your own. Instead start telling yourself that the only thing that grows really well on its own is a tumor. Take hold of yourself, and push yourself to sit tight and stay put. Put aside all thoughts of leaving him and instead accept on faith that your marriage is forever. View your relationship *as if* it is going to last. Have what is in effect a play date with permanency.

It helps to accept that being married involves giving up short-term excitement for long-term stability. Accept that dull and safe routines are beautiful, that feeling deeply is better than being on a perpetual high, and that a ball and chain makes a smarter anklet than an identification bracelet.

Even go to the opposite extreme and experience the joy of clinging to him, the closer the better. Do lots together and you just might discover that creative merging is not your problem but your goal. Will you become just too dependent on him? For some people that can be a problem. For gay men with a fear of commitment, that can be a solution. Stick with this plan until you stop feeling stifled and crushed and instead find yourself getting used to this new, higher level of relationship.

Step two involves making overcoming your fear of commitment a joint effort. Don't try to get through this alone. Ask your partner to work with you. Ask him to just accept that you are a high-maintenance item, and that being married to you won't be easy. Tell him, "I may have problems, but together we can do something to solve them." Tell him exactly what you fear, and why, and ask him to help you overcome your anxiety. Tell him how sensitive you are and about what. Make a list of things that cause you to become particularly anxious, hand him the list, and ask him not to do anything to you on the list. For example, ask him not to make fun of or otherwise invalidate what positive feelings you are able to express. Ask him to reassure you, if it's the case, that he will always be available to you, ever faithful to you, and never leave you. Tell him that pulling away from you even a little is a big problem for you and tell him how much you long to instead be pulling together. You will probably find that, almost paradoxically, getting your fear out in the open can help contain it.

Paulie distanced himself from Roberto to cope with a constant fear that Roberto would reject and leave him. He had nightly dreams of being separated from and unable to get to Roberto because he didn't know Roberto's telephone number, or because the trains weren't running, or because Roberto didn't answer his phone. One night he dreamt that Roberto was on a bus tour to the south and not ever coming home, and another that he was swimming in the ocean far off the coast getting ready to drown beyond Paulie's reach. In real life, when Roberto was even a few minutes late coming home, Paulie began to fear something terrible had happened to him, like a fatal automobile accident.

One day Paulie screwed up his courage and told Roberto of his dreams and of how they reflected his fears. As it turned out, instead of Roberto's complaining that Paulie was too dependent for his liking, Roberto told Paulie that he actually enjoyed having someone who never wanted to let him out of his sight, and that he was touched by all the concern for his well-being. Roberto liked the new Paulie so much that he hung around him all the time just so that he could have even more loving coming his way. Instead of feeling resentful and demanding his space, he reassured Paulie that he would never even think of leaving him. Roberto and Paulie had become codependent, and moreover they discovered that they liked it that way. The last time I spoke to Roberto he said, "What's wrong with having a lover who always wants to be around me? Who needs me? Who says, 'I'm always there for you' and never wants to leave me? I don't mind my cat constantly trying to sit on my lap, so why should it be a problem when Paulie does that very thing?"

Getting your fears our in the open can prevent the vicious cycle of mutual distancing, where you protect yourself from rejection by being remote, until he thinks you don't like him, when, feeling rejected himself, he pulls back from you, until you feel even more rejected, and protectively pull away from him even further—as the wrong messages fly and cross in an O. Henry-like series of misunderstandings where you sell your toupee to buy a watchband for the watch that he sold to buy you a visit to the hair salon.

It prevents what happened to Malcolm and Shawn: Malcolm became convinced that he should get a divorce when in fact he just feared being married. He would proudly tell himself and remind everybody else too that he was an independent guy who didn't really need anyone. But underneath he wasn't so much independent as he feared being dependent. Being an old hand at getting himself left, he was now hedging his bets so that he would have another guy in case his present one walked out on him. Not surprisingly, by pulling back he created the very circumstances that he most feared. That's because his partner Shawn, sensing that Malcolm was pulling away, would begin to pull away himself, defensively. Ultimately each partner thought he was defending himself against the other, though he was just defending himself against himself.

Step three involves trying to understand your fear of commitment through and through. The following is a compendium of some of the commonest reasons gay men fear commitment.

Perhaps you feel that opening up to someone, anyone, is dangerous and likely to backfire, though what is more true is that you can never be too thin, too rich, or too loving, because while sometimes partners leave you for loving them too much, more often partners leave you for not loving them enough.

Perhaps you fear being overwhelmed by closeness because as a child you were trapped in a situation you couldn't get out of, and now that you are an adult, the first chance you get you bolt from any situation that reminds you of that. When Darrell was a child his parents would come on too strong and to the point that he would constantly dream of fleeing. Now as an adult the fleeing fantasies get revived whenever he feels that someone is infantilizing, criticizing, or controlling him just the way his parents used to. When that happens, he thinks about leaving for California, where he keeps a professional license just in case, although he is certainly never going to move there. His fear of being tied down emotionally also originated in a childhood experience in the operating room where he was literally tied down to be anesthetized, so that now he feels uncomfortable in anything restraining, which of course to some extent all relationships are.

Marriage offers thousands of opportunities like this to breathe new life into old problems. A better idea than just allowing your old fears to resurface in new garb is to make, and use, a two-column list: on the left what you fear, and on the right, why you don't have to be so afraid.

Another common basis for the fear of commitment is a need to maintain your identity intact to the extent that you feel it is terribly dangerous to let anyone close to you and inside your heart. You view your beautiful desirable partner as a Trojan horse who will destroy who you are if you let him past the hard self-protective shell you have so carefully erected around yourself. Here's a better suggestion: instead of locking yourself away in your fortress, build a bridge over the moat you have dug around your personal castle, and after carefully checking the inside of that

Trojan horse for hidden surprises, that is, after doing a careful assessment of who he really is and what he is really about, open your gates, and just welcome him home.

Perhaps you fear commitment because you fear merging and need separation because you believe that being close means almost literally disappearing into the body and soul of your husband, as if he is going to engulf you or swallow you up. Yes, relationships to some extent do swallow you up. But for me that is not their problem but their chief advantage. Yes, in relationships the boundaries between you two blur and dim. You may even grow frighteningly alike to the point that you cannot always tell the two of you apart, the same way people come to look like their dogs. You give up some of your hard-edged gay sophisticated individuality to the point that you can even become sort of a faceless mall maven. But that's excellent. See you on the lower level near the lovely cascading fountain and together we'll toss a penny in and wish you and your relationship well. Everyone told me and Michael not to move to a loft together because in one room we would be on top of each other. Wow, bring it on, exactly. If you must grow on your own, do that outside of your relationship. Back at home, decide that the best idea is to stop growing on your own and start growing together.

Perhaps you are unable to commit because you fear being controlled. You stay independent in order to be able to tell yourself, "Look ma, no handcuffs"—that is, "Ha, ha, you can't dominate me in any way, small or large." So when he calls you during the day just to say hello you respond not by being pleased to hear from him but by being annoyed that he is following you around and nipping at your heels.

Perhaps you fear commitment because you have been hurt in a past relationship. So yours is not a fear of rejection but of "re-rejection," making it difficult for you to develop and sustain basic trust. You fear he will walk out on you just like the last one did. So you, like anyone else who has had a really bad experience, start scanning the horizon so hard that you actually begin to hallucinate your destroyer coming in. A better idea is to tell yourself that not everyone is the same, and instead of making premature assumptions about him make a list of ways he differs from all the others in preparation for giving this new one the good old college try.

Perhaps serious jealousy is an important reason for your fear of commitment. Our Paulie held Roberto to extremely high standards about sexual fidelity, to the point that he attempted to monitor all of Roberto's sexual fantasies. He felt extremely threatened if Roberto so much as looked at another man. His jealousy was so painful that he said to himself, "Better out of this relationship than having to lie on this bed of nails." Like Paulie, you may feel you would rather be out on the street on a smooth cardboard pad than at home lying on an uncomfortable spiky mattress. If this is you, see if my chapter on jealousy has something in it for you.

Perhaps you are unable to get close and commit because you feel guilty about being successful in anything. If so, try being a little kinder to yourself. Start by telling yourself that you deserve to achieve as much and to feel as happy as the next guy.

Perhaps you fear commitment because you want to be a man and you equate being a man with being a mountain man, a loner type meeting nature by himself in a test of strength and mettle that only the strongest and most powerful can endure and survive. At the same time you believe that marriage emasculates you. Your positive feelings make you blush, and you fear that if they should get out your friends would laugh at and humiliate you for being queer, and this in the older sense of the term.

Perhaps you are a very competitive person who fears being second best in anything at all, so that you always have to be the winner. Now you want out every time your man does something to enter a spotlight you want all for yourself. Even when the dog comes over to him first you begin to feel envious and want him out of the picture so that you can dominate your little frame.

Perhaps you are just too selfish to make the sacrifices any relationship requires. If this is you, you don't so much fear commitment as you want it all.

Perhaps you fear commitment because you are the sort of person who cannot stick with any stand at all you take. You can no more commit to one man than you can decide which tie to wear or which job to accept. You don't so much fear commitment specifically as you obsess about everything generally.

Of course, your fear of commitment may be to an extent socially-determined. Perhaps having bought into gay (and straight) society's pigeonholing of domestic chores you fear that being a homebody makes you into a fagola. Perhaps having bought into the cachet gay society so often assigns to being free, independent, wild, and crazy, you refuse to commit in order to confer a certain standing on yourself in a community of free men. True, a string of successful sexual conquests does give you bragging rights. Your buddies act proud of you and that makes you even prouder of yourself. But what is that worth? After they give you the gold star, what do you actually do with it?

Now that you have found out where you are really coming from you are in a better position to change your route. Here's how. Make a two-column list. In the left-hand column of the list, put down the reasons I just gave for fearing commitment. In the right-hand column of the list, put down your thinking about whether or not that reason applies to you, and if it does, try to see that you are dealing with a myth rather than a fact, a fear and a fantasy rather than a reality. Put down the worst that can really happen should your fears come true. For example, if you panic and feel overwhelmed by closeness, so what? You won't faint, and you won't melt. Also put down what the alternative is. Would you rather feel anxious or lonely? Now you have it all laid out for you in black and white, and instead of being driven to act for reasons you don't understand you can make a better, more conscious, decision about what is actually best for you.

Step four, which can easily be taken in tandem with the other steps, involves dealing with your fear of commitment by facing commitment directly. The worst way to overcome commitment anxiety is to avoid it. The best way to overcome it is to allow yourself to be terrorized for a bit so that you can get used to, cope with, and bravely overcome it. Always remember that the best way to get out of cowering in a corner is to pole vault directly to the top.

Step five involves not doing things to get yourself actively rejected. So often people who say they fear commitment because they fear rejection forget that rejection isn't necessarily something they experience passively. Rather so often they court it actively, and even consciously. Don't proudly wear that T-shirt that says, "I don't get headaches, I give them." Yours is certainly a problem with a solution, for the "best" way to avoid being rejected is to avoid being rejecting. Don't say, "I want my space." That is just another way to tell him to get lost. If rejecting you is just what you fear he might do, why are you encouraging him to do it?

Here's an exercise I suggest you try. Stand in front of the mirror and tell yourself, "I want my space." Hear yourself talking. Keep in mind the effect that your words are having on your partner. Ask yourself, "For heaven's sake, what am I saying?" and, "Mirror, mirror on the wall, am I not the unfairest of them all?" If you are being honest, you will realize that he won't think, "He is afraid of loving me," but will rather think, "He hates me." Now he will feel lonely and isolated and begin to fear you are planning to leave him. Next he will become uneasy, take precautions, and decide to have that little something on the side, just in case, which of course only makes your fear of committing to him more rational, and therefore much stronger.

In conclusion, don't make too much out of the minor annoyances associated with marriage to give yourself an excuse to get out of your commitment. Don't look to getting a divorce so that you can be a "you" growing on your own. I have never yet seen a formal study that says that being alone is good for your emotional and physical health. Nobody grows on his own, anyway. What people do on their own is wither. You can accomplish all the growing on your own you need to do while growing together.

Now, if it is your partner who is the one who fears commitment, remember that the general positivity principles I outline in chapter 4 may not work so well to get him out of that zone. In fact they can have the reverse effect—by scaring him. Positivity can be too overwhelming for partners who fear closeness. The secret to handling a man who fears commitment is not pure positivity but moderation and flexibility. Okay, here playing a little hard to get can actually help you get what you want. So, treat your commitment-shy partner like that fish that needs reeling in. Don't just drag him in with a steady pull. Instead give him play to avoid losing him. Pull him in but don't yank him too hard to the point that you scare him away. Instead gradually build up his confidence and trust so that he can move closer comfortably without feeling that he is the subject of a behavioral experiment who gets a shock every time he tries to get near you. Grant him a measure of freedom, while at the same time letting him know that he can count on your always being available to him. Soothingly reassure him that you are doing everything you can to make him feel comfortable. Make sure that he knows that his fears about you are just nothing more than bad dreams, so he can just go ahead and wake up, putting his dreams aside in favor of reality.

9

Danger Zone 5: Getting Past Self-Absorption

In my experience complaints about partners ranging from "He hates me" to "He turns me off sexually" often boil down to "He always puts himself first, me last, is insensitive to my feelings, and doesn't care about my welfare."

The following checklist is offered to help you decide if these complaints apply to you, if, in other words, you wander off into the self-absorbed zone from time to time, hurting or even killing your relationship with a degree of self-involvement that makes it hard for you to become truly involved with him. Most of us display at least some of the following characteristics on at least some occasions, so you should only consider yourself deep in this zone if you check off more than four items on the list. Yes, it's difficult to admit to having some of the characteristics I describe, making it particularly hard to develop self-awareness in this area. But since the problem is potentially serious and not at all difficult to correct, I ask you to try to be especially, even brutally, honest with yourself here. And please remember that though I tried to avoid throwing brickbats at you, I couldn't find a way to discuss your self-absorption and at one and the same time to send you bouquets of roses.

- My appearance is top priority. How I feel mostly depends on how I look.
- If there is anything that makes me feel really great about myself, it's

having people tell me that I don't look my age.

- Being cool and chic is important to me. After all, I have a reputation to uphold.

- To me, style is more important than substance. Though he loves music, I won't let a stereo in the house because I can't stand looking at all those ugly tangled wires.

- I feel like I am a big nobody unless I have a husband who is a really big somebody.

- I have very high standards for what I want in a husband.

- I want a husband who makes a splash, someone handsome, reliable, rich, and very well-endowed, so that I can brag about him and show him off to my friends to make them envy me.

- I only feel whole when I have an adoring appreciative audience.

- I often talk about myself in terms of my personal and professional achievements. Ask me "How are you?" and forget about "Fine." Instead be prepared for a recital of my latest theatre engagements along with my positive reviews.

- When people don't put me up on a pedestal and worship at my feet I become very vicious.

- I often put on age-inappropriate displays. I plan to celebrate my big 5-0 by hitting all the discos and staying up all night on stuff.

- The only car for me is a sports convertible. I know they won't notice that my comb-over is flapping in the wind as I drive it but will instead think, "Boy, I envy him, that's panache, and boy, I would love to have him and make him, and what he has, mine."

- If he loved me better, he would cater to me more.

- No one, least of all my partner, can ever satisfy my needs completely.

- I have temper tantrums when he doesn't give me my way absolutely and gratify me fully—by remembering my birthday, my anniversary, and that I need brand new kitchen appliances, and that I need them now.

- I sometimes feel that my marriage is there just to nourish me.
- I do what makes me feel good, and if it feels good I do it.
- What he feels isn't important; it's what I feel that counts.
- The only way we get along is if he puts up with me exactly as I am.
- Disagreeing with me at all is exactly the same thing as defying me completely.
- Criticizing me at all is exactly the same thing as hurting me deeply.
- I see anything he says to me that isn't a compliment as a criticism.
- We have to do things my way, not his. I divorced my last husband because we couldn't agree on when to throw the old spices out before they tasted like hay, or how quickly we have to put food back into the refrigerator after serving it so that it doesn't spoil and we have to throw it out.
- I would never consider giving up my career for my marriage. You mean the other way around, don't you?
- I believe that his bad habits defy me personally, so that when he doesn't make the bed in the morning or doesn't make it right, leaves his clothes all over the floor, sleeps too late, and wears clothes that are too loose even though I asked him not to, I suppose that he does these things not because he has a problem but to spite me.
- I don't feel completely loved or wanted unless I have a little something on the side.
- Because conquests give me not only nourishment but also status, I always kiss and tell. What's the point of *not* telling? If I did that, how could I enjoy the admiring look in my friends' faces and the envy in their green little eyes?
- I cannot accept blame for anything that happens in my marriage. Whenever things go wrong he, not I, is the one at fault.

- Empathy and altruism are for suckers. Put myself in his shoes? Not those dreary pumps.
- I often think that I am better than he is. For example, I have all the taste in our family, with my decorating skills far superior to his, so it's only my expertise here that keeps us from making some terrible design mistakes.

Most everyone, gay or straight, goes in and out of the self-absorption zone. As I was writing this chapter I thought of something I did when I was sixteen years old. I was at a summer camp on Cape Cod and I decided to leave our compound on the sly and hitchhike to Provincetown at the end of the Cape. Great idea for me, but when the camp owner discovered I was missing, she quite naturally panicked over my fate and the possibility of a lawsuit, although not necessarily in that order.

Gay men (straights, too) in this zone give only when there is a chance of getting. The opposite of self-sacrificial, they think mainly and almost exclusively of themselves, so that they have little or no time, energy, and emotional commitment left over for their partner. They don't see the need to gratify, and don't get much pleasure out of gratifying, their partner. In this zone they become unempathetic individuals who self-centeredly go after what they want without taking what their guy wants into consideration. In this zone they maintain their identity regardless of how doing so might affect their partner. They want to be free as a bird no matter how their partner might feel about their flight path. They prefer to fit their marriage to their needs rather than the other way round. They want the benefits of marriage without its constraints, the gains of a relationship without its pains, the "for better" always, and the "for worse" never, and the "love" without the "honor and obey." To make matters worse, it's hard to get some of these zone-prone gay men to change their ways. If you try, they confound constructive with destructive criticism, accuse you of straitjacketing them, and see your setting limits on them as proof that you don't love them.

Forgetting that he and John were a couple, Steve would make John invisible by saying, "I bought this" when it was really "We bought it," "I have this" when it was really "We have it," or it is "mine" when it was really "ours." When John spoke Steve would not even listen to what he had to say. John would say something important to Steve only to have Steve two days later ask him a question that indicated that Steve hadn't heard anything at all that John had said. Then Steve would excuse himself when John said, "But I already told you that" with a cutting comment like, "I cannot listen to *everything* you tell me."

Steve would also demand that the two of them do what he wanted them to do without first asking John how he felt about that plan. For example, though Steve knew that John had a fear of flying he still insisted that they tour the world, although John just wanted to collect mushrooms or bird-watch close to home, or at most travel to a nearby beach or hike the local mountains.

On a somewhat less lofty note, Steve would spew popcorn on the floor when he ate it, and leave the screen door open when he went in and out, letting the bugs in and the cat out. When John asked him to stop he would reply, "I don't care about a few kernels or flies," and besides "I hate that cat." John was making a reasonable request, but Steve was bridling, thinking that John was picking on him—and, in his view, no one picked on him, because according to Steve, Steve was perfect, with his blemishes illusory and his personal problems nonexistent.

It all ended with Steve feeling just too sexy for John, then becoming promiscuous, having convinced himself that anything would be better than what he had at home, and that anyone in his shoes would run around on his partner because if they didn't they were just wasting their time being faithful to nothing and nobody.

Getting out of the self-absorption zone starts with **step one**, which involves realizing that you are in it and need to move on. Recognize that yours is a deep zone where you win small but lose big. You gain an advantage here or there but ultimately you lose by putting your entire relationship in jeopardy.

Step two involves lowering your opinion of yourself. Stop thinking that you deserve to have anything that you want and start depriving yourself of what is good for you but not for your husband and your relationship. Stop thinking that you are just too sexy for the man you have and accept that he just may be as sexy as you are, and sexy enough for all practical purposes.

Step three involves doing things his way some of the time, not your way all of the time. Relationships may not be fifty-fifty, but try to make yours at least sixty-forty by being more flexible and accommodating. That leads us to the next, most important, step of them all, step four.

Step four involves becoming more empathic and altruistic. I previously discussed empathy and altruism in chapter 4, but here's some more on these topics presented in the new context of narcissism, which I define as the opposite of empathic altruism. *Empathy* involves using yourself as a barometer to test the interpersonal atmospheric pressure. Put him in your shoes so that you can better understand his needs and fears. If you fear closeness, maybe he does too, so back off a little. If you need to be free and hate being controlled, maybe he also feels uncomfortable about being tied down, so loosen the reins. Become sensitive to his hidden agendas. Read between his lines to get into his head to know what he is thinking without his having to spell it out for you exactly. Translate everything he says into what he really means. What does he really intend to convey when he complains that you always want to do things your way? Hint:

suspect that he hates to be ignored, thinks that you are rejecting him, and is telling you that he dislikes feeling powerless. Automatically fathom what you might be doing to upset him and, before you carry things too far, voluntarily, and immediately, pull back. Also, be sure to respond to his nonverbal cues as well as to his verbal communications. The best thing many guys can do for their marriage is to become proficient at mind reading without simultaneously becoming adept at being paranoid.

Being empathic isn't as hard as it might seem. A big part of it involves just understanding human nature. We all hurt in the same place and in the same way. It's human nature to need love, approval, attention, and respect, want to be independent until we need a little help, want to be dependent until we feel too enclosed, both desire and fear control, tend to be at times too possessive and at other times not possessive enough, and tend to become overly competitive with our partners even when we know perfectly well that being adversarial is being the opposite of loving. Also, most of our anger isn't really about being mad. It's about being disappointed, or scared, so that angry guy of yours just might be a scared little child who rages less because he is furious and more because he is frightened.

Again as previously discussed, *altruism* involves giving him what he wants and needs even though that means sacrificing some of your own pleasure and gratification. If your man is very sensitive about being left alone, and you want to drive somewhere to get the morning newspaper, and he looks at all uncomfortable as you begin to walk out the door, what about saying, not, "I'll be back in a few minutes," but, "Do you want to go with me?" Going out to walk the dog? Always ask him to go along with you so that he doesn't feel that your dog comes before him.

As an altruist you want the best for him, even if second best is all that is in it for you. You think, "After all, this is my man, so I will love him more and myself less." Then you choose the road that leads to his happiness, even though yours goes the other way. You make his well-being more important than your own, his needs your goals, and his preferences your marching orders. You put his family before you and you put him before your family and your job, so that you don't visit Mom and Dad on the holidays leaving him home alone or, getting married to your job, do too much overtime at work when he is the sort of person who likes you to be home at night as much as possible.

Pat had an old lover, Jim, whose father was a well-known musician. When Jim died he left behind boxes of papers, among which were some letters written to his father by prominent musicians of the time. Pat treasured these and wanted to keep them, less because they reminded Pat of his old lover than because they had some intrinsic value. But Pat's new lover Bob wanted Pat to sell the letters as a show of faith that he was putting the old relationship in the past. So that's exactly what Pat did, because he felt that his relationship was more important than his documents.

Like classical music and he likes disco? Leave the disco on. It will only kill you if you have killer thoughts about it, like "What happens to my identity if I let him have his way" or "If I let him get away with this, what will he want to get away with next?" or "Fair is fair, and he is being disrespectful of my desires and why should he always be the one to get what he wants?" or "He listened to a half-hour of crappy disco, now it's my turn for a half-hour of Beethoven the Sublime."

Altruism also means catering to your guy and that means giving up catering to yourself. Look at it this way: there is a finite amount of narcissism that each relationship can tolerate, and you don't want it to be all yours all the time. If you don't already know what you have to do to cater to him, ask him directly, and ask him to be specific. Tell him not to be embarrassed to say what he really wants, and ask him not to say "no" to something that really matters to him.

Put maintaining your identity second by allowing him to maintain his. Once again, an identity is a self-attitude created for multiple purposes, especially for self-approval, to get the admiration of others, and to achieve social status. Up to a point, a fixed, high-profile identity is okay, but what constitutes your ideal self needs to be aligned with his expectations of what constitutes an ideal husband. Don't complain that your marriage takes away your individuality and interferes with your healthy development. Instead, to avoid turning both of you from people who should cross into people tracing parallel paths, give up anything about your individual identity that interferes with the development of your healthy marriage. Let your individual identity slide to the point that his emerges so that both of you begin to develop an "us" identity where your relationship, not yourself, becomes the most important part of "who I am." Always remember that the ABC of marriage is to Always Be a Couple, and think and say "we" and "us," not "I am out of money today" or "My family said that…" but instead "We are broke" and "Our family commented that…"

Step five involves giving up copping this and that attitude. Don't be one of those stuck-up husbands, more interested in stroking themselves than him, whose attitude leads them to divorce court. Here are some narcissistic attitudes that have the potential to turn you from Mr. Right to Mr. Just Been Left.

You think you are too good for him. Don't lord it over your husband. Maybe you actually are an A-Gay who has in fact been to the manor born and has become so accomplished that you are entitled to all the great things rich, gorgeous, and successful people like you should have. But when married you are part of a constellation, not the only heavenly body in the sky. He wants to have some star quality too, so don't constantly push him out of the spotlight so that you assume your position center stage.

You think you deserve to have your married life consist of one fabulous experience after the other. Don't feel that the ordinary things aren't good enough for you. Content yourself with everyday pleasures. Make that weekly shopping excursion "Just one of those fabulous flights" that Cole Porter might have called, if he had lived today, "A trip to the mall on gossamer wings."

You always have to be the one on top. Don't think that he always has to be the one on the bottom. Jim picked the man he married, Bruce, for, as he saw it, being a great big nobody, an unworthy person who shone only in Jim's reflected light. Then out of a need to always be the Alpha Dog, he put Bruce down and in his place every way he could. One day Bruce, no longer able to tolerate being a mere member of the pack, decided to go out and become a big somebody on his own, so he started looking for another husband, one who would share the spotlight with him instead of always trying to keep him in his shadow.

You need him to be a trophy husband. Don't think he is only there to make you feel like a winner. His chief purpose isn't to improve your self-image, as you drag him around to impress your friends, family, and therapist with what you got. It's the rare partner who can live day after day just being an ideal showpiece in his husband's perfect showplace.

You are so perfect that he shouldn't or can't ever tell you what to do. Don't complain that your guy is a smartass husband always giving you marching orders when in fact he is only trying to help. Once when Joe was having irregular heartbeats his partner, Arthur, a doctor, told him to cut down on his coffee intake. True, Arthur's tone and manner were somewhat authoritarian and intrusive, but Arthur's motivation, to help Joe feel better, was entirely admirable. Still, Joe, unable to distinguish advice, suggestion, and legitimate request from assault and control, could do no better than to condemn Arthur for being too judgmental, for interfering, and for making him subservient.

You feel you should always be able to speak your mind. Don't think that it is perfectly okay to get things out of your system no matter how much you hurt his feelings. Don't think that you should always be able to run roughshod over your partner's ideas, beliefs, and feelings. Many partners I have treated, concerned that unexpressed anger will eventually build and grow until they blow up, and told by the experts that being able to get angry is a good healthy release that clears the bad bile out of their system, had a hissy to purge their soul and clear the air. Only they discovered to their horror that instead of clearing the air they had cleared their room.

You are too independent for the good of your relationship. Don't be one of those men who, afraid of getting close and sharing, is always complaining that their partners are taking their independence away from them by overwhelming them with love. Fear of commitment and its devastating effects on one's partner and marriage were discussed at some length in chapter 8.

You put your things before your husband. Don't insult your lover by making it all too clear to him that your house is more important than your home, that is, than your relationship. Don't be one of those men who dream of getting a divorce just so that you can sit there surrounded by the gewgaws you love that, as soon as you get rid of that intruder, will be no longer half his but all yours.

You are a perpetual victim. Don't be an injustice collector who blames everything bad in your marriage on your husband. Don't be one of those men who make sure that all their friends know about their marital strife, and who the real troublemaker in the family is, and of course it's not you. Perpetual victims always do everything right and their partners always do everything wrong. We hear, "If I hit him it is not because I am by nature a violent person but because he provoked me to do it." If they don't do something right (and according to them they are rarely wrong) it is because their partners led them into temptation and caused them to make a mistake. So as they see it the only thing wrong with them that needs to be changed is their circumstances, and the only thing right about their partner is that he deserves to be congratulated for going to therapy to find out what he is doing wrong.

You play the part of the closet straight. Don't be one of those gay men who never really accept being gay. These are the guys who look to a straight remnant in themselves out of a sense of guilt related to moral issues as well as for real reasons such as wanting to have children. In their guilt about being gay they forget that almost anyone can reproduce, but not anyone can redo the garage to make it into a delightful cozy den. Such men often go on to blame their lovers for making and keeping them gay. They then make trouble in their marriage so that their partner leaves them and now they can get married "the right way," the way they thought they should all along, and as a bonus, the way that would most please their parents and the society they live in.

You play the part of the wannabe saint. Don't be a guy who lets his moralistic preoccupations distance him from hubby. David, whose identity was as an animal lover, focused on how his partner Colin didn't want pets and, thinking that only selfish people have no pets, used this as a (trivial) disqualifier to put a wedge between himself and Colin.

You are a "blood is thicker than water" queen. Don't make it perfectly clear that your family always comes first. Men who do this hurt their lover and their relationship by putting their parents and siblings 100 percent before their husband. They are always too busy to spend any quality time with him because that means taking time away from spending it with mother. These men are often mama's boys in two ways. They are dependent people afraid of growing up, and actual victims of a possessive punitive critical judgmental family that their lover couldn't compete with even if he had a large dowry, an exceptionally large sprawling mansion in the country, a long, very beautiful, very flowing, yet at the same time very modest veil, and an important bloodline going way back to the Viqueens.

You are the "Miss Perfect Bitch" perfect bitch. Don't think that now that you are married you no longer have to pull in your claws. Joel would always criticize where he and his husband Phil were and the people who were there with them. Just recently at dinner, Joel took off on a couple who entered the straight restaurant they were in—on him, for dying his gray hair red and combing it up from the sides to make it look like he had a full head of hair, and on her, for wearing ghostly white makeup making her look like something right out of the Addams family. He often made funny but critical jokes at the expense of dinner companions who were just trying to enjoy themselves and his company. His sarcasm and negativity began to grate on Phil, who didn't want to constantly have to hear about "all the fat-ass people who live in this town" and because, as he listened to Joel's dishing other people, he became all too aware of who was next.

You refuse to be like Mr. Mom in any respect. Don't be one of those men who make just too much out of the gender identity issues associated with the daily tasks of any relationship. Such men can't even do the dishes without feeling that it's too feminine. They forget that knitting is not a symbol of who they are but just a way to make mittens to keep his beautiful hands warm. Don't be one of those men who distance themselves from their guy because they view closeness and intimacy not as an integral part of a good relationship but as a sign of passivity, submissiveness, weakness, and femininity—then go cruising because as they see it that is a man thing to do.

Now, if your partner is the one in the self-absorbed zone, try to set limits on his self-concern, self-interest, and self-preoccupation. Point out the problem and tell him how it adversely affects you and your relationship. Remind him that there are two of you here and that you count too. Be consistent, firm, and patient until he gets the point. Meanwhile give him time to change. It takes a while for anyone to fall out of love with himself. Never criticize or threaten to leave him if he doesn't go along with the limitations you set on him right from the start. That will only make him defensive, and instead of decreasing his self-absorption it will mobilize it further.

10

Danger Zone 6: How Not to be Uptight

Some partners are laid-back guys who let very little bother them and don't carry on about a whole lot of things. Other partners take everything to heart and much too seriously. They take precautions in the absence of danger, and atone for sins and apologize for crimes they haven't actually committed. Such men have many good qualities. They do the budget and make it balance; they keep the house clean by taking off their shoes so that they don't get dirt on the new white carpet; they save soap by plastering the old shard onto the new cake; they never waste money by using an outside bank's ATM machine even if that means burning gas traveling to the mother bank; they are satisfyingly precise about the distinction between a powder room and a half-bath; and they don't kiss just anyone to avoid getting bad germs and bringing them home. But they aren't so great to have around should they cross the line and become a player in the neurotic games of protect, avoid, regret, and retract. Now they begin to drive their husbands crazy. If this is you, you can't get a dog because it might pee on the rug. Your hubby can't put his feet up on the sofa without your picking them up and putting a cloth under them. You can't have sex without his taking a shower first so that he doesn't dirty you or the bed sheets. In the end your anxiety is contagious, and he winds up as much of a nervous wreck as you are. So one day you get a little note left on your bureau, neatly typed, without spelling errors, and folded perfectly right down the middle: "Meet me at divorce court, because that's the only way that I am ever going to get some peace."

Because all of us have our little quirks and tics, you are only in the uptight zone if you check off ten or more of the items in the following list:

- I feel vaguely anxious all the time, as if nothing is exactly the way I want it to be.
- Not a day goes by without my worrying about something that probably isn't going to happen, or if it does happen won't matter.
- I worry about the same thing over and over again and I can't stop myself.
- No matter how many times he tells me "Don't worry, it's not that important" it doesn't get through to me.
- Not a day goes by without my having a major crisis about something minor. I sweat the small stuff, as I make one big deal after another out of little things.
- We are incompatible because though I worry constantly, he doesn't worry enough (or at all). I feel that one should worry about something before it occurs, while he feels that one should only worry about something after it has actually happened. He is too relaxed and laid-back for my taste. I may need a tranquillizer but he looks like he just overdosed on one.
- I make him as uptight as I am by telling him about and involving him in my worries.
- Of course, little things mean a lot. Little things are like specks in the eye—they don't amount to much by themselves, but they can easily ruin your day, or even your whole life.
- I focus not on winning big but on avoiding losing small. Paying all

that attention to the little things means I don't pay much attention to the big things. To me a stain on the carpet can seem even more important than a stain on our relationship.

- I am a pessimist who thinks that if things are going well now, something bad is lurking around the corner and, as if by magic, is bound to happen to screw everything up. For example, for fear of cursing it, I will never brag about something good I hope will happen before it actually occurs.
- To get along with me he has to meet my standards exactly and to tolerate my whims completely.
- I am the perfectionistic type who must have things clean, neat, straight, and even, and all the time. My more sophisticated friends call me anal. My less sophisticated friends call me a version of that.
- I try to never make a mistake, and I expect that he won't either.
- I focus on the little things he does wrong, never on what he does right.
- I tend to be fastidious, even prissy. You may not believe it, but after where my mouth has been Saturday night I still complain about a little spot on the water glass in our favorite restaurant at Sunday morning brunch.
- Above all I love a bargain. Can you believe: I got this four foot by four foot carpet remnant for only $3.99? That's less than twenty five cents a square foot!!!!
- Even though we have enough money I insist we economize all the time, to the point that sometimes he says he can't stand all my penny-pinching.
- I am always early, sometimes too early, for our appointments. Then I complain if he hasn't already arrived because I figure that if he really loved me he would be there waiting for me so that I didn't have to hang around waiting for him.

- I cannot stand one little thing out of place in our house. So you often find me turning the tchotchkes around, lining them up, and arranging and rearranging them until they look just so.
- You would think that I am predictable, but I am not. Though I am very clean in certain ways I am dirty in others. As perfectionistic as I am in some areas, I often mess up in others. For example, my suit is perfectly pressed but my underwear is all wrinkled because I left it in the dryer for three days. While the living room has to be picture-perfect, our bathroom looks like a garbage dump. So what? Who of real importance is going to care? And anyway, it's a bathroom, not a day spa.
- I feel that sex is dirty. I am dead set against certain forms of touching and licking, so don't make me do them. I would get into the missionary position if I could do it that way, with a Bible in one hand and a washcloth in the other.
- I demand that my man be like a statue, a sex object without a body, one of those fantasized men who don't even pee or dump.
- I have an anal awareness of my husband. I keep thinking of his passing gas, and that disgusts me, and makes me want to find someone cleaner, who isn't like that. When we first got married I put him up on a pedestal because I thought that he was a statue. Now I see, and am disappointed to find, that he has a body just like everyone else. I particularly hate the unpleasant smells he makes in the bathroom. The fan and the deodorizers just don't do it for me.
- I believe that we all should be ashamed of our bodies and as much as possible try to deny that we have them.
- I am a very moral person, sometimes to extremes. I happen to know what the high road is, and I expect him to travel it with me, exactly, and follow the path I have laid out for him, precisely. I will never let him off the hook for the one time that he bought a bootleg CD

(that's dishonest, after all) and for the times he ran the dog on the beach when the sign said no dogs until off season (that's breaking the law, after all). As far as I am concerned, being a little bit immoral is like being a little bit pregnant.

- I am a very guilty person full of thoughts about sin. When it comes to issues of sin, I can outpope the Pope. If I feel I have done something wrong I atone, over and over again. For me, gay love is always saying you are sorry, and a lot more than once.

- I have lots of rituals and completing them is more important to me than making him comfortable and happy. The keys have to be hung on the hook we installed for them near the door, and if they aren't, and he just throws them down on the table, it drives me wild and crazy, and I have to pick them up and put them where they belong. Then I go back to check to see if I actually did that, several times in fact, until I can sit down reassured that in our beautiful house there is a place for everything and everything is in its place.

- After he washes the dishes I have to wash them again to make certain he got all the dirt off with the soap and all the soap off with the water.

- I can't leave home unless I know the house is neat and clean.

- If something is broken I have to fix it before I can get on with my day.

- I check on things constantly to see if I ruined them.

- I am careful about my possessions even to the point that I actually mess them up. For example, I covered all our furniture with plastic so that it didn't get stained, only to later find out that all this time it was rotting underneath. The day we removed the plastic the sofa fell apart completely.

- I hate it when he refuses to accept and tolerate my little peculiarities. It makes matters worse when he pokes fun at or ridicules me or tells me to cut it out already.

- I do many of these things because I am dissatisfied with us. I straighten up the house constantly because I feel there is something that needs straightening up in our relationship and in our lives.

Some gay men like their partners in the uptight zone; others feel that they make bad companions and worse lovers. I have had lots of friends and patients who muddled through marriages with such men, even though they took a lot of the fun out of life by taking almost everything too seriously. They were the guys who always built a wall of worries from extreme concerns about nothing and engaged in trivial pursuits at the call of trivial prompts. These men were like Rich, an A-one uptight worrier. He would clean and mop all the time, worry about whether one of his possessions might get stained, continuously rearrange the end tables to get the room looking just right, and constantly walk around closing the cabinet doors that Steve had left open. For one birthday he asked Steve to buy him a present of a new dust mop, and for a major birthday the gift he most desired was a second vacuum cleaner so that he could leave one upstairs and not have to schlep the only one they had up and down from the first to the second floor every time he wanted to clean the whole house–which, not surprisingly, was several times a week.

Rich was totally unable to just enjoy being happy. He constantly worried about Steve's leaving him. More than once he would ask Steve if he were good enough for him or if he were planning to look around for someone better. Rich was also a man of too many principles, the sort of person who believed strongly in right and wrong dichotomies and enforced his beliefs through whining, nagging, and arguing. For example, though Rich worked at home and Steve went out to work, Rich still demanded that Steve do the breakfast dishes, and reminded him constantly that that involved more than putting them in the dishwasher—it also involved taking them out after they were done. Rich put great store in Steve's meeting that request, which then became a philosophical sticking point for the entire relationship, as in, "If you won't do that for me, what will you do for me?" and "You would do this for me if you really loved me," and "You should do this for me because I did that for you," and "You should do that for me because it's the right thing to do."

However, when Steve asked Rich to do something, also on principle, Rich wouldn't do it. Rich, full of control issues, felt that giving into Steve in any way meant being his lackey completely. Rich was an excellent cook and he and Steve always loved to have people over for dinner, but Rich refused to invite people over in advance. Instead he would wait for them to drop by, then only at the last minute ask them to stay. He told everyone that that was because he liked to do things spontaneously, but it was really a fear of passivity and being controlled that drove him to be so impressionistic. When Steve complained, Rich refused to change because that too meant cooperating and that meant yielding and that meant being someone's slave and that meant being feminized.

Rich was also a negative pessimistic person who only focused on the bad things Steve did, never the good. Rich created a composite picture of their relationship out of the last bad thing Steve did to him. He would always ask himself, "What good thing has he done for me lately?" So if Steve did something he didn't like today, Rich felt as if Steve never, ever did anything good at all. Rich not only never overlooked anything bad that Steve did but also created bad things from the good by putting a negative spin on Steve's neutral actions. Once he blew up at Steve because Steve was ten minutes late coming home. That's because it was not about the ten minutes or so that he had to wait, it was about the supposed symbolism of the act. Rich saw Steve's being late as a sign that he didn't love him enough to be on time. It didn't seem to matter that Steve was held up due to an accident on the parkway and tried to call but couldn't get through because Rich was yakking on the phone to one of his cronies about how Steve never came home on time.

Rich was also rather cheap, because he was always worried about balancing a budget they had enough money to not really need in the first place. Rich had driven their car for months without sound brakes because he was waiting for exactly enough money to come in from his monthly paycheck so that he could have the cash on hand to pay for the brakes without having to put a charge on his credit card or take out a car loan for a new car. As far as Rich was concerned, borrowing even a small amount of money was completely against his principles, a kind of immoral aligning himself with the devil. Of course, Rich was selective about what his principles were. He was perfectly comfortable with the one about never being a borrower or a lender, but somehow the principle about its being a good idea to always be able to stop in time on a busy highway completely eluded him.

Rich had a number of annoying rituals. Each time they left the house they had to go back to make sure the stove or the gas fireplace was off. Rich drove Steve crazy because when they were eating dinner at someone's home when the host was doing the dishes Rich had to butt in to give them an extra wash to make sure all the soap was off. In public places he would go to the men's room then disappear for over fifteen minutes, locking the door and creating a long line because he would wash his hands, then touch something on the way out, then, feeling he had contaminated himself, have to wash his hands again, then touch something on the way out, and so on.

When it came to making love, Rich was so uptight that he virtually had to have a church organ playing during sex. He felt that uninhibited sex was dirty and made him into a slut. Rich couldn't have much fun with sex. He was too busy making rules and avoiding touching the bad, or as he put it the "dirty," parts to enjoy fondling even the good.

If you are in an uptight zone like Rich, consider the possibility that you are driving your husband crazy and move into a different, more relaxed, place. A good start is to stop being such a perfectionist. Anticipate that the less you demand the more you will get. Stop trying to have it all and instead lower your expectations from excessive to reasonable. Learn to live with your whole package, which certainly includes the possibility of not liking some of its parts. Don't ever dissect your marriage alive into its components then fail to put it back together again to form a composite whole that includes the good that softens the bad. Don't paint the big picture only out of his vices; paint it out of his virtues as well. Dismiss his little quirks. Overlook his minor defects. He is just the way he is and you can love him in spite of and even because of his flaws. Give him an opportunity to do a lot of things you don't like or approve of. Everyone makes mistakes and everyone has a bad day now and then. Nobody's 100 percent, 100 percent of the time. If he makes a mistake, tell yourself that "It is not important, I will learn to live with and get over it." Most things really don't matter so much anyway.

If you are having trouble seeing your relationship as a reasonably good whole, try making a two-column list. In the left-hand column of the list write down your man's flaws, as you perceive them to be, and in the right-hand column write down his virtues, and if you are being honest you will almost certainly see that the virtue side is longer than the flaw side. Rate the importance of each item on your list by giving it one to five spaces depending on its *inherent* significance, not the significance *you assign* to it. One space is trivial, five spaces is important. Now you can weigh the items according to how significant they are based on how much space they do, or should, occupy. That way you can avoid making too much out of the one-liners and focus all your attention on the headliners. You can avoid blowing minor things up way out of proportion, which means you will be less likely to have your marriage survive the big stresses only to succumb to the little ones.

Now try to overlook a lot. Remember that to get something important (a lifetime of marital bliss) you may have to give up something else, something of major or something of minor importance like a perfectly balanced budget or a beautifully ironed bed sheet. Don't, like Randy, feel anxious when he doesn't fully satisfy you. He can't meet your every need or cater to your every whim. Randy, in his younger days, got quite upset about his marriage when, as happens in any marriage, little things went wrong. Randy's lover Arnie liked the country, and besides, his job kept him there. But Randy constantly complained that he hated living in the country because it was keeping him from living his preferred city lifestyle. Particularly troubling to Randy was that it was impossible to throw out the garbage because, unlike in a New York City apartment with its easy access to the trash chute down the hall, here getting rid of the garbage meant having to travel to the dump five miles away. Believe it or not, this is what Randy called the straw that broke the camel's back. That's what I call a small straw, and it's sitting on an already pretty bad back.

Become a less critical, more charitable person. Don't be one of those guys who always jumps to negative conclusions about everything your husband does when there is a more positive explanation for what he just did. Give him the benefit of the doubt wherever you possibly can. Does he change his mind a lot? Maybe he is contradicting himself, so that yesterday he says he wants to eat there but today he says he wants to eat someplace else. But which is it: inconsistency is waffling; consistency is the hallmark of the narrow mind; or what difference does it make in the first place? Don't hurtfully condemn him for not being able to make up his mind about something and stick with his decision. Instead, being more positive than that, congratulate him for being flexible.

And certainly don't jump to negative conclusions about unfinished actions. Here is an illustration of what I mean by that from outside of the marriage realm. Once at checkout time in a supermarket I put a shopping basket on the floor in the aisle as I fumbled for my shopping card. The checkout person assumed that I was going to leave it there and warned me that I was about to trip someone up. Of course, I wasn't going to leave it there, I had planned all along to move it after I stopped fumbling, and she should have known that, and held her tongue until the whole incident played out. In parallel fashion, at least give hubby a chance to finish what he is doing before you complain about what he has done.

Consider the effect your worrying may be having on him and stop constantly torturing him (and yourself) with this and that inflated concern. Don't make such a big deal out of everything. So he is being messy while cooking. Does that really mean that you have to clean up after him as he goes along? Can't it wait? He likes his little sinful pleasures? That doesn't mean you need to be like Charles, who just because he went to bed early and got up early on Sunday morning felt that his partner David needed to get going at seven in the morning with him. David on his part liked to stay up late on Saturday night and sleep late on Sunday morning. A healthier Charles would have been perfectly happy puttering around the house until David got up, but that wasn't the point. The point was that Charles decided that sleeping late was being lazy, so he got David up because he felt he was committing the unpardonable sin of sloth.

Forget advice that you need to grow up. Maybe you just need to become more like a child again by becoming a little less serious. You need to be like my Michael who when he spills something dreadful on a new shirt says, "Life happens" and "Life goes on" and "It will all come clean in the wash." Then, when it doesn't, it's not "Mea culpa" or "What a loss," but, speaking for the moment to the shirt, it's "Adios buster; off you go to a worse place." I will always remember how relaxed and great it is to be around Michael. I can't ever recall exactly a single shirt he ruined and had to be replaced.

It often helps worriers to understand the why of their inflated concerns. For one thing worriers make symbols more important than the real thing. But if he doesn't pick up after himself it doesn't mean he is literally trying to dump on you. He can forget your anniversary without that meaning that he is forgetting you. More likely than not there is no sinister meaning to be attached to the bathrooms always being a mess, or his putting wet towels on the bed, or his not making the bed, or his dropping his popcorn kernels all over the place and not cleaning up after himself, or his putting down his wet drink and leaving rings on your beautiful armoire. These things are a little annoying, but they don't mean that seriously meaningful clouds are gathering.

When Steve recommended Rich get a new car instead of just repairing the brakes, he was trying to be helpful and to keep Rich from getting into an accident. Rich however thought that Steve's request was symbolic of how Steve needed to give him marching orders, and protested that "nobody controls me." The actual situation didn't concern Rich as much as it should have. It was as if Rich didn't mind going off a cliff as long as he was still free when he hit bottom.

If your guy is the one who has cornered most of the market on being uptight, forget all that you have learned about how to push his buttons. If he is a neat freak, don't use poor personal hygiene or carelessness about your appearance to drive him up a wall. Don't get spots on your clothes and deliberately dribble when you eat just to annoy a lover who likes you prissy pristine. Don't wear last century's styles just to upset your fashion maven, and don't put away the razor, grow stubble, and look grubby just because he likes you clean-shaven. Never leave wet towels on the bed or the closet doors open with the lights on to deliberately rile him. If he is a fussy individual, don't complain about his fussing. Instead, remember that you can't usually beat him, so join him, or at least try to meet him halfway. Anyway, there is nothing wrong with wanting to make things just so. If he wants to clean the floor with a cotton swab, let him, and don't scream that he is overdoing it. Just lay in a supply of cotton swabs and make sure that he doesn't make tiny little streaks. No harm done as long as you at least have a little time left over to eat, sleep, and have sex.

When it's true, try to reassure a worrisome lover that he really has very little to be concerned about. Did he start thinking he left the lights on at home just as the lights went down and the overture began at that new musical comedy you waited a year to see? Reassure him that the cost of electricity is not that much for just a few hours, and that the likelihood that the bulb will burn the shade and start a fire minimal to nonexistent. If he is the type who as soon as you get ten miles from home cannot remember if he left the stove on and wants to go back to make certain that you didn't, go back, or at least consider appointing a neighbor to be on tap to check things out after you leave, and even to be there to take an emergency call should the worries start and your reassurances have no effect.

Try finessing little gathering disputes to avoid having big blowups. Is he a control freak fighting about who is paying for what and who is contributing more to the kitty, not because it's about money but because it's about power? Start your own savings plan for your present and future personal needs, and then give him the rest of everything you got. Try tricking your stubborn partner into doing exactly what you want him to do. If you want him to meet you at two o'clock and he is the kind of person who is always late, tell him that you want him to be there at one o'clock and sit back and relax expecting him to be there right on time—your time, not his. Trouble is, with some guys that only works once or twice until he catches on and makes the necessary adjustment so that he can continue to be just as late as before.

Try to remember that from stubborn people the more you demand the less you get, and vice versa. Stubborn people say, "Let me know what you want; that way I can know what not to give you." They won't do something because you want them to do it even when they want to do it too. They withhold things in order to get a rise out of you. So instead of getting caught up in the action, don't tense up, and just sit back, wait, and watch him relax.

11

Danger Zone 7: Dealing with Paranoia

In both my personal and professional experience many divorces take place because one or both partners are hypersensitive, suspicious, critical, blaming, jealous individuals who by always thinking the worst turn a loving relationship into an adversarial situation and, acting accordingly, make their guy into the very monster that, though he never was, they nevertheless begin to imagine him to be.

Of course, all of us when we are in love enter the paranoid zone at least a little and from time to time. That is because love itself is close to paranoia. Love routinely makes people thin-skinned and suspicious. The more in love people are the more likely they are to begin to imagine themselves hated, plotted, and schemed against. That's why when I ran the checklists to follow past a number of gay men most of them found themselves answering "Yes, frequently" to many of the items, and winding up with a positive overall reading. If that happens to you, take the result not as an indication that something is necessarily seriously wrong with you or your relationship but as a heads-up alert, a warning that you are close to entering a danger zone and should immediately take steps to back off to avoid getting too far into it, thereby destroying what could have been a permanent loving relationship of a lifetime.

Each of the four checklists that follow reveals a different paranoid sub-zone: hypersensitivity; suspiciousness; blaming tendencies; and possessiveness and jealousy. I have separated these subzones out for purposes of clarity, but in real life most gay men who go into one of them also go into the others, either simultaneously or consecutively.

Subzone #1: The hypersensitive zone

- I am extremely thin-skinned—easily hurt, especially by what I perceive to be his negativity and criticism.
- He has to constantly walk on eggshells with me if he is going to avoid upsetting me and riling me up.
- Unless he says something very positive I read it as extremely negative, even before all the facts are in.
- I think that if he doesn't love me all the way it means that he hates me completely.
- I hear the bad things he says about me and notice the bad things that he does to me but the good things he says and does elude me completely.

Subzone #2: The suspicious zone

- I often feel that my partner is planning to cheat on me or is actually doing that already.
- I often feel that my partner takes advantage of me financially. When I begin to think that he is scheming to get my money, I call up the bank, sometimes several times a week, just to make certain that he didn't withdraw all my savings and empty our joint accounts.
- I often feel that he is saying bad things about me behind my back.
- I often feel that he is scheming to leave me when I least expect it.
- We can't have a domestic partnership—I fear that if I sign those

papers he will rob me blind.

- I often think that my partner can read my mind and know exactly what I am thinking, both about him and about other men.
- I know I can read his mind and figure out exactly what he is thinking. I'm good at putting two and two together, although he claims it doesn't always add up to four.
- Just because I always pretty much know what he is really thinking doesn't make me paranoid. It just makes me especially perceptive. I am not so stupid that I can't read between the lines and, like my version of the song says, tell that the "Styptic on your collar means you've been untrue." His collar was closed when he left this morning and open when he came home tonight. I know why that happened, and I even think I know with whom.
- I suspect that his compliments about me are secret criticisms of me. If he tells me that I look great today, I think he is really telling me that I looked terrible yesterday.
- Basic trust is for fools. You've got to cover your rear end at all times, even, or especially, at home.
- I need constant proof that he is not being unfaithful to me. To avoid arousing my suspicions, he should be available to me when I want him to be. He should always be accountable to me 24/7/365/52/50+, so that I know what is going on with him at all times. For example, if he says he is not going out he should always answer the home phone when I call him up, and he should always leave his cell phone turned on so that I can reach him when there is something to "discuss."
- When he tries to defend himself against my accusations I know that it just means that he is hiding something from me.
- I actually like being suspicious of him because it gives me an excuse

to do what I wanted to do all along. I imagine that he is cheating on me so that I can respond with, "Whaddya expect me to do, sit home while you are running around? I'm not dead yet" and cheat on him in return, either to get there first, or to pay him back for what I have a pretty good idea he did to me.

Subzone #3: The blaming zone

Gay men, of course, don't have the corner on playing the blame game. They aren't the only ones who make external Satans responsible for their own devilish actions. But some gay men do play the blame game full time and in spades. Gay men who go into this, the blaming, zone become highly critical people. Theirs is a "not me" view of their relationship that consists of cursing out their partner for everything that goes wrong in their partnership. If this is you, as you see it, you are always completely innocent and pure and he is always and completely guilty and foul, so that out of your mouth come tumbling such big ideas as "If I act like a bitch it's because you piss me off." If you are sexually impotent, you blame hubby for being a sexual dud. If you are cheating on him, you insist that you only wander because he doesn't have what it takes to keep you interested, or because he is thinking of cheating, or has actually cheated on, you first. If you are ashamed of something you did, it is not because you ought to feel guilty, but because first he made you do it and second he is being too hard on and overly judgmental of you for having done it.

- I rarely take responsibility for what goes wrong in our relationship. As far as I am concerned, when they say a relationship takes two that doesn't apply to me, or to us.
- When I *do* do something wrong, I don't feel guilty, only provoked.
- I raise some fair questions about our relationship but always in an angry way, so that we fight about, instead of trying to resolve, our problems.

- I am unwilling to cut him any slack, put up with much, or coddle him at all. After all, he's a big boy now, and old enough to get his act together.
- I feel resentful of him a lot, and often over very small things.
- I provoke him so that we can fight and it can look like he started it.
- I provoke him to do something wrong to me so that it's "Gotcha, I have you exactly where I wantcha."
- I believe that assigning blame, that is, trying to figure out who started it and who did what to whom, is more important than maintaining the peace, and being loving and affectionate. Who started a fight is more important to me than what we are fighting about, or how to stop the fighting and settle our differences.
- I constantly complain that he doesn't take my side even when he cannot possibly do that because I am not completely right, or am in fact all wrong.
- I disavow my own guilty feelings by attributing them to him—that is, I project my own disavowed feelings onto him so that I can avoid seeing myself just as I am. My anger with him shows up as a fear that he is angry with me. My desire to cheat on him shows up as a fear that he wants to cheat on, or is actually cheating on, me.
- What I condemn him for is for those things I don't like in myself. When I blast him for being up to something it's because I feel sheepish about wanting to do, or having done, that very same thing.
- I am attracted to trouble in our relationship. I have a vested interest in making my negative prophecies come true so that I can say "I told you so, I said all along that this wouldn't work."
- I like a good fight because it makes me feel real and connected.
- As an abused man I may have black and blue marks around my eyes, but it's worth it because just by virtue of being the wronged party

and holding it over him, I now hold all the power in our relationship.

- I frequently and without good reason get angry with him, and I can even become physically abusive to him when I start thinking that he has wronged me.

Subzone #4: The possessive/jealous zone

In my experience as a psychiatrist, extreme possessiveness and jealousy cause more gay relationships to come to grief than almost any other interpersonal issues with the possible exception of sexual performance problems and problems related to sexual and substance addiction. Extreme possessiveness and jealousy account for much of the suspiciousness and blaming that cause gay relationships to fail, partly because they create their own quagmire, for if you are impossibly and irresponsibly jealous of someone it can drive you apart by provoking him to behave in a way pretty much guaranteed to make you even more jealous than you already are.

Going into the jealous zone often starts with your getting the hots for everybody and his cousin. Next you feel ashamed of yourself and begin to feel that you have to do something to make yourself feel less so. So you rid yourself of your forbidden desires by reattributing them to your partner. You start brooding about the possibility that he is looking at, and for, other men, until you become convinced, whatever the reality may be, that he is actually cheating on you. Now you become pathologically jealous, and often take the next step and start cheating yourself, feeling justified because what does he expect, you aren't getting it, you are only giving it back.

In effect you have projected your own sexual desires onto him, making you the innocent and him the guilty party. It is as if your thoughts have boomeranged right out of your own head and come bouncing back at you unchanged in any way except in direction. Your cheating heart has become his cheating heart because you have transplanted yours into his body. In your own way you have become like the classic homophobe, a closet queen who deals with his own forbidden and unacceptable homosexual desires by queer baiting and bashing, putting out the flame in others' pants in order to extinguish the fire in his own. You are doing what a colleague of mine just did. He put his mother in a nursing home because she was totally obtunded from a stroke. Then, out of a sense of his own guilt, he completely misinterpreted her blank stare at him as her looking at him with hate in her eyes for his having institutionalized her.

Antoine, an openly gay man in the jealous zone, dealt with his own forbidden desire to cheat by condemning his partner Myron for cheating on him, then by taking steps to make sure that that it didn't happen again. Antoine found himself following Myron around just to make sure that Myron was heading for the supermarket, not for the super. As it turned out, it was Antoine who was attracted to the super, and assumed that Myron was thinking along the same lines. Not surprisingly, Antoine became a difficult person whose accusations turned Myron off to the point that Myron actually started cheating on him, because Myron was thinking, "Well, if he is going to blame me for it, I might as well do it anyway," and "Well, what a bitch; I really need some R and R—somebody to cut the curse of that one and his constant pecker checks."

Several checklists follow. I first try to help you determine to what extent behaviors on his part that may not be entirely out of line nevertheless still throw you into the jealous zone. Study my list of gradually escalating behaviors generally found to make partners jealous, then yell, "That's too much" when you go beyond what you can accept, having reached your threshold of pain—indicating that you have attained a level that you just can't handle. The lower your threshold the more likely you are to be a jealous type, although drawing the line exactly between "okay" and "not okay" is close to impossible because you can't pigeonhole feelings of jealousy that scientifically. Of course, the likelihood that you are going into a jealous zone increases the more you feel that most or all of the vignettes to follow describe your fears exactly.

- He looks at another man on the street when he is walking along just to make sure he won't run into him.
- He speaks to another man at a party, says more than hello, looks as if he is enjoying himself, is excited (not bored like you think he should be), does not look uncomfortable as if he cannot wait to get away, and says more to him than he said to you all day.
- He has close male friends at work, and they go out to lunch together.
- He goes out with the girls and you think he is going straight and you will lose him completely.
- As you go by the porno shop, he sneaks a peek in the window.
- You call him at work and he doesn't answer the phone so you worry that he left for a noonday delight.
- He wants to go for a walk by himself, and you live in a gay ghetto.
- He says someone he sees on television is cute, or beautiful, or sexy.
- He goes out with his guy friends at night, leaving you home and you don't like it, and you think he is going to cheat on you with them even though they are all straight.
- He walks around in the nude with other nude men in the men's locker room at the gym.
- He spends an overnight at a convention away from you—at least he *said* he is at a convention.

Now try to determine if you *think* in a jealous mode. You think in a jealous mode if more than two of the following describe you adequately:

- I am very sensitive to the possibility that he likes someone better than he likes me.
- I often think that he is wandering sexually.

- I often worry that he is going to leave me for someone else, someone better.
- I cannot learn from experience so that I still think he is cheating on me when I have had proof, over and over again, that he is not.

Next try to determine if you *behave* in a jealous fashion. You behave in a jealous fashion if more than three of the following describe you adequately:

- I check his wallet or go through his pockets looking for incriminating scraps of paper.
- I check his clothes for telltale rumples.
- I call him at work to see if he is really there, and if he is out to lunch I call again to make certain he has returned on time (then, when he gets home, ask him where he really was).
- I check the caller ID for phone calls that came through when we were away, looking for calls to him that I cannot account for as business calls or calls from mutual friends.
- I get to know some of his friends not because I like them but so that I can check up (spy) on him.
- I constantly ask him whether or not he loves me and me alone.
- I don't allow him to talk or write to an ex-lover.
- I don't allow him to invite an ex-lover over.
- We don't go to all-gay parties—we only go if lesbians are there to make sure that the guys don't get out of line.
- I tell him that fair being fair I will cheat on him if I ever have any reason at all to think that he is going to cheat on me.
- I cheat on him because I have become convinced that he has already cheated on me.

Jealousy can be nonsexual as well as sexual. *Nonsexual* jealousy is about his being close to anyone, even his mother. This kind of jealousy is characterized by your thinking he is completely ignoring you in favor of someone else who is not a potential lover, as when at Christmas dinner his talking to his mother some of the night means he isn't saying a word to you all night long. Many in-law problems are really the product of this sort of jealousy, disguised and rationalized in such terms as, "Sure, I hate her, doesn't everyone hate his mother-in-law?" You might be surprised at how much fight-producing stress really comes down to "You pay more attention to/love him/her more than me."

Sexual jealousy can be either warranted (provoked) or unwarranted (unprovoked). *Warranted* sexual jealousy can be the product of a partner's cheating, the outcome of a polygamous arrangement gone awry, or the result of one partner's sadistically trying to make the other jealous just for the fun of it—for example, as when one partner sensing the other partner's vulnerability just drops that little hint that he is having lunch with an ex-lover, but don't worry, he isn't planning to add the "s" to the "ex."

Mild unwarranted sexual jealousy is quite common. In fact, it is an unavoidable and even desirable part of working long-term relationships. One desirable component is its protective aspect. Mild sexual jealousy keeps a relationship healthy and helps it survive. Two men cannot make it together forever if they aren't at least a little bit jealous of each other. So, if he is a little unreasonably jealous of you, that's good. It means he cares. It is a sign that he loves you, as in "I only worry about what you might be doing because I adore you and I want you to do it only with me." Therefore, you can make a big mistake by telling him to stop being at all jealous of you, for on one level you are telling him to stop loving you. Also, if you are a little jealous of him, that's good too. It means that he still excites you.

So, mild unwarranted sexual jealousy doesn't need to be challenged and corrected. Instead it needs to just be accepted and built into your relationship to the point that it doesn't matter quite so much. As a paradigm, we live in a very noisy neighborhood in New York City. My neighbor is bothered by the noise, because she doesn't like who it is coming from ("screaming faggots," as she so delicately puts it). I don't hear it at all because I don't care. So, if you don't let mild sexual jealousy bother you so much, you just might not hear it at all.

However, *severe unwarranted* sexual jealousy is a different matter entirely, and something that has to be dealt with. **Step one** involves not putting basic trust to too harsh a test. For example, when you are just getting started in a relationship consider the possibility that it might be best for the two of you not to live in a gay ghetto, especially if one or both of you are very good-looking. At the beginning of their relationship when complete trust hadn't yet been established because they didn't know each other very well, Brent and Darrell agreed that it was a good idea to move out of a section of Chicago which had more gay men than straights. (There were other reasons to go, but this was one of the main ones.)

In the beginning Brent didn't trust himself a lot more than he didn't trust Darrell. So he took steps to control the enemy within by managing the enemy without—by moving to a blue-collar town where there were fewer available men to be tempted by. Then afterwards they pretty much isolated themselves in the country. They found that an additional advantage to living in the country was that the isolation brought the two of them together and made them closer to and more dependent on each other—but not to the extent that that became a problem. After a few years they eventually did feel comfortable enough with each other to reclaim their *pied a terre* in Chicago, and now they enjoy it immensely. And back at the ranch, they moved out of the country and into a little town with a large gay population where they could have a small but select group of friends. (The rules about third parties, which I discuss in chapter 14, still apply, no matter how old and firm a relationship is).

Why take a chance? It is always a good idea to apply one of the dieter's tricks that actually works: remove all tempting food from the house so that the goodies lying around don't cause your basic instincts, hard enough to control under the best of circumstances, to boil up and take over. Heed the diet guru's advice to follow—just replace the concept "food" with the concept "sex": "Do not hang around people who eat too much, but instead hang around people who watch their diet, are slim, and exercise a lot."

Unfortunately, when it comes to deciding if jealousy is warranted (provoked) or unwarranted (unprovoked), the rules to tell you exactly when you should and when you should not get jealous aren't very good. Maybe you should not want him parading around in the nude in close quarters with other nude men. As with many other things, there are borderline cases where no one can say "This is right and that is wrong." As one of the above checklist illustrates, each of us has our personal comfort zone, and each of us has our personal limitations. Some men are natively more sexually jealous than others without being pathologically so. Their's is a jealous style that is an integral part of some people's personality. This can be extremely difficult to influence under the best of circumstances.

Step two involves identifying your jealous zone, using the above checklists, and after separating the sense from the nonsense dismissing the nonsense from your mind with the help of step five, to follow. The nonsense consists of two types of distortions. The first involves unwarranted fears arising strictly in the *here and now* about his abandoning you and leaving you completely alone; his controlling you; or his being spirited off by a third party. The second consists of unwarranted fears arising from *contamination of the present by baggage from the past*, so that in the here and now you might become unduly afraid of your guy's leaving you for someone else because back then when you were young your mother had another child whom she seemed to prefer over you.

Step three involves just waiting for your jealousy to dissipate on its own, instead of letting it all come out. You should not impulsively blurt out hurtful things like, "I hate you because I think you are cheating on me," even if you are only saying that because you are in a temporary snit and the idea just popped into your head as a convenient way to convey what are just momentary feelings of anger.

Step four involves just admitting that you are a jealous type and asking him, even pleading with him, to humor you. If you deny it and continue to act jealous anyway, you will come across as petty and difficult. If instead you just admit it, he might be willing to help you handle it—hopefully by constantly reassuring you that you have nothing to be jealous about. If he doesn't do that, maybe you don't have something to be jealous about. Maybe you just have someone to be disappointed in.

Step five involves reducing your jealousy by putting a positive spin on your guy's behavior. Put as good a face as possible on what you are tempted to first view as a bad thing, giving it a positive not a negative twist. Here's an example of what I mean by putting a positive spin on things. I planted two dahlias and when one didn't come up I started screeching that there was something wrong with the second one and that the plant store screwed me. Michael, however, putting a good spin on what I saw as a really tragic situation (I didn't have enough to worry about at the time), said that the second one was just on a different schedule. So we were patient, and just today the second one is peeking up and out, giving the lie to my having badmouthed a spunky little piece of vegetation from a plant store run by honest hard-working burghers.

Make a journal. On a page write down what you fear, and on the left- and right-hand side of the page write down the two alternative (negative and positive) realities. Then underline the negative one in red (a warning to you!) and the positive one in black and review your entries frequently. If you review your journal when you first wake up, you are likely to have a better day. If you review your journal when you're about to go to sleep, you are likely to have fewer nightmares

Here is a sample journal entry. "What I fear: he is cheating on me." On the left, underlined in red: "He mentioned his new assistant twice in one week. I wonder why? Could it be that he is getting ready to have an affair with him? I wonder if he is cute, and maybe interested too." On the right, underlined in black: "Of course he talked about him a few times. People always talk about work when they come home, and he doesn't talk about him any more than he talks about anyone else on the job, and besides, when is he doing all this cheating? He always comes home on time to me, so it's really unlikely that anything at all is happening."

Now, if your partner is in the paranoid zone, if he is a hypersensitive, suspicious, blaming, jealous type, why not try walking on eggshells with him? It's worth the attempt if only because it's better than walking alone. Here are the steps involved in walking delicately with great, even exaggerated, sensitivity, combined with humility.

Step one involves slavishly following the rules of polite society with him. Polite society was born to avoid ruffling the feathers of hypersensitive suspicious blaming jealous people. Polite society takes all the old-fashioned fundamental values to heart, and makes its guiding mantras such clichéd maxims as "honesty is the best policy" and "do unto others..." The lesson from polite society is always to take his feelings, particularly his irrational feelings, into consideration, keeping one eye forever open as to whether you are insulting him seriously and hurting him deeply. Bad: you are too fat. Good: let's go on a diet together.

Alf knew that Farley was a very jealous man, yet he insisted on parading around in the nude with other nude men in the showers at the gym, which was mostly straight, but as Alf knew, you never really know. Farley was very upset about this, and got very depressed, yet he wasn't really comfortable saying anything to Alf, because he knew that Alf would snap at him, accusing him of cheating. Nevertheless, the anger mounted up until Farley couldn't handle it any longer, at which time he blurted out what the problem was. How did Alf respond? Even though he knew how upset Farley was, Alf still insisted that there was nothing wrong with playing the lead in the peep show. Maybe Farley was overdoing it by getting so upset, but Alf should not have gone for Farley's jugular. Instead of accusing him of being irrational, he should have cut him some slack, left room for his jealous feelings, and given him credit for at least being honest and open about them.

Step two involves taking his worries and complaints seriously and instead of devaluing them, and him, reassuring him that he has nothing to worry about.

Step three involves taking his side whenever you can so that he doesn't ever think that you are against him. Never defend "them" over "him." Err on the side of saying "You have a right to be upset" rather than on the side of saying "Get over it, you are too sensitive." Try to avoid "You are imagining things," in favor of "I see why you are responding that way, I would too." Certainly don't be like Saul who when his lover Roland legitimately complained about Saul's father, Saul shot back, "You are not half the man he was."

Step four involves never giving him an actual reason to distrust you. Start by always asking for his okay before you take important action on your own. Don't invite people over without checking with him first, or buy major items for the home or for yourself without involving him in the purchasing decision. That way you will be symbolically reassuring him that everything you do you do upfront, not behind his back, and with him in mind, leading him to make the connection between minor things like inviting and buying, and major things like screwing around. This step involves never being less than completely truthful about anything and everything, small or large. Being less than truthful about small things will certainly raise questions about whether or not you can be trusted about the big things. It also involves always being accountable. Give him proof, not an excuse. Show him exactly what *is* going on so that he can stop worrying so much about what *might be* happening.

Step five involves not provoking him at all, but especially about sexual matters. If you must push buttons, at least don't push the sexual ones. Do you, knowing that he is a jealous type, nevertheless try to make him feel that you are seeing someone on the side, and to boot are getting pretty good at making him worry about that? If the answer is yes, stop bringing home little scraps of paper with cryptic notations on them, or leaving them in your pocket for him to find when he does the laundry. Stop receiving and accepting phone calls from mysterious strangers. Don't disappear saying you are one place only to have him discover that you are in another. This is not only about sex, it's also about trust, and it's certainly about kindness.

Step six involves graciously admitting it when you are wrong both to keep the peace and to avoid bending his mind. Defending yourself when your actions are indefensible confuses him and you don't want a paranoid guy confused about reality. Always remember that even paranoids are right some of the time. Chris talks to a neighbor and Walt complains that they are getting just too chummy, and wants to know exactly what is going on. Sounds like paranoid jealousy, doesn't it? But just which neighbor is he talking to? The one who Walt knows frequently makes passes at Chris?

Apologies are a really great way to throw cold water on hot feelings already there. In effect you are offering the tender underbelly to stop an attack. Saying "I see what I did and understand how it must upset you" will almost always stop an argument or at least keep it from developing into a fight.

Step seven involves bypassing his jealousy, just not hearing it in the hope that he will simply get tired of and over it. The methods for bypassing emotional encounters are discussed throughout this book.

Step eight comes into play if he is actually cheating on you because he decided that you did it first when you didn't do it at all. That involves deciding whether or not to forgive him and whether or not to set limits on his future behavior. Make your decision swift and precise. Your goal is not to torture him with uncertainty about where you stand, or to exact revenge. It's to damage control the situation.

Step nine involves, are you ready for this, actually being a little jealous, or becoming a little more jealous, of him. Men who are themselves jealous actually like to have their partners jealous of them. That way they don't feel so silly and so alone. Your jealousy makes them feel wanted, and it provides him with consensual validation ("you are that way too, I see") that keeps him from feeling he is nuts. So when an old lover of his shows up at the door, don't say, "I don't care about what you did before we met." Say "It may be foolish, but that really bothers me." That will at least reassure your guy that you are attuned to such matters and in the same place as he is, at least enough to know where he is coming from, and understand what his hurting is all about.

12

Danger Zone 8: Overcoming Excessive Dependency

Some of the responsibility for the dissolution of gay marriages belongs to the all-too-common tendency gay men have to put too high a premium on personal independence. For one thing, instead of loving wisely and well they confuse a healthy desire with an unhealthy behavior, as they confound bonding, closeness, and intimacy with clinging, overwhelming, and strangling. For another, they follow the crowd and view committed long-term relationships as the essence of boorish and uncool, as well as antithetical to the true meaning of being gay—then they get a divorce and move on just to do what they believe to be socially acceptable. As a result they wind up sacrificing a lifetime of joy, comfort, and stability in order to be politically correct and gain approval from their peers.

The following checklist is offered to help you spot unhealthy dependency—to distinguish being wonderfully intimate from being overly close. But remember: in this checklist it's not so much a matter of *kind* as it is a matter of *degree*. For all of us are dependent, and being *too* dependent is a matter of how much, how long, how constant, and how troublesome the effect on your partner, with the latter differing from person to person and from situation to situation.

- I always have one eye open and a measuring stick in hand trying to determine whether or not he loves me, and if he does, whether or not he loves me enough.

- I compare his love to some ideal amount I wish that I could have but fear that I don't have and will never get.
- My greatest enemy is being isolated from him. If it were up to me I would never let him out of my sight, even for a moment.
- I hate doing things by myself. I am only interested in doing things with him.
- The slightest distance between the two of us makes me feel completely abandoned.
- I constantly check up on him to make certain that he isn't running around on me and planning to leave me. When he is just a few minutes late coming home I worry that he is out with someone else and that that's going to be the end of us, or that he has had an accident on the road and that I will be widowed and then, because I don't have any other family, be all alone for the rest of my life.
- I start to worry that he is going to leave me at the first sign that he requires just a little breathing room and asks me to give him some.
- Everyone complains that I cling too hard to him. I want a man who lets me cling to him. I admit it, I'm like a vine: I don't grow well without a lot of support.
- I am afraid of my anger because I am afraid of losing him if I get just the slightest bit pissed.
- After squabbling with him I keep him in my sights less out of love and more out of fear—to make certain that he isn't going to leave me because we had a little tiff.
- I am not very enterprising. I never initiate anything in our relationship. I let him take over and assume the lead.
- I see myself as a tiny little mouse who can only survive if I don't call too much attention to myself by making too many demands on him or otherwise flashing any sort of neediness.

- I am always cooperative, compliant, conciliatory, and passive, and I don't mind being that way even if it does involve sacrificing a great deal of my individuality.
- More of the same is my watchword. What I have now is what I want forever—a dull day the same as the last dull day, the same as the dull day before that.
- When I get to feeling abandoned I start cruising for sex, really for love, to fill what seems to me to be a bottomless pit. At such times I can be insatiable. That's the nice thing about the baths. You can run dry, but you can never run out.

You are not in this danger zone if yours is a *healthy* dependency. Your dependency is not *unhealthy* just because the two of you happily feel that you simply cannot live without each other, and that if something bad ever happened to the one it would take the other years to get over it, if he got over it at all. As one of our healthily dependent neighbors in essence put it, "We have decided that when it's time to go we will both take a flight and jump out of the plane together." This may be an impractical solution to a practical problem, but it's a great, if overly idealistic, spiritual position.

Yours is not an unhealthy dependency just because the two of you are mostly inseparable. Give you space? You like to be crowded. Your definition of space is nothingness and emptiness. Your inspiration is not the Montana Big Sky but the New York Rush Hour. You just love him too much to want to spend a lot of time without him. When you two get home from work, you stick together, and when you have to go somewhere, before you leave you ask him if he wants to go with you.

If Michael sees that he is going to be late getting home from work he asks me to join him at the hospital for the hour or so that he plans to be delayed. (He works right down the road so I can get there in just a few minutes). As he puts it, that way we can at least be together sooner. When

Michael used to be on duty on weekends I joined him for lunch. When he had to travel to do some outside work, whenever possible I would stay at his side, really in the next room, waiting for him to be finished. Are the two of us dependent? Yes. Are we *overly* interdependent? I don't think so, because at least for me being close to him keeps me from feeling lonely. Some people would feel trapped in and stifled by such a relationship. He and I personally wouldn't have it any other way.

A big part of a healthy dependent relationship is the willingness to sacrifice "you" for "him." You willingly put up with a lot, and gladly put him first. You happily lose small so that you can win big overall. Another big part is your willingness to gladly exclude troublesome outsiders at the first sign that they are trying to invalidate your marriage—people such as the ones who criticize you for putting all your eggs in his basket. Instead of going along with them you recognize them for the disenablers they in fact are—envious people who deal with their own shame about their loving feelings by condemning those very same feelings in others, dishing you for being too dependent and condemning your relationship as overly close to cover up their personal anxieties about being intimate, or their personal grief about the losses they experienced in their own lives.

This said, some dependent/codependent relationships *are* problematic, and you are possibly entering a danger zone when:

Your dependency brings your partner down. Robert's retirement from his nine-to-five job destroyed Bill's career as a writer, for he was hanging around the house all day long and constantly whining that he wanted to travel. Robert made it impossible for Bill to do his work. Bill's work deteriorated, he got a few rejection slips, then he decided to retire completely—prematurely as it turns out, because he had so much left to say.

Your dependency is a way of expressing hostility, not love. When this is the case we call the result "hostile dependency." In this zone you hang around him all the time, less because you love him and more because you are afraid that he hates you for what you just recently said or did and to look for signs that you are safe. One day, as soon as Morton walked through the door five minutes late, he found Warren quietly simmering with rage for the longest five minutes of his life thinking that Morton didn't love him enough to be on time. Instead of having a cold drink waiting, Warren hit Morton with "Your being late makes my day too long" and "If you loved me you would be certain to leave work on time." Next, Warren, out of a sense of guilt and a fear that he would be banished for biting the leader of his pack, hung around Morton the whole night, much as a dog that just nipped his master hangs around and hopes for a forgiving pat. Morton loved Warren, but for now Morton could only feel that his guy was less like a husband in need of a lover and more like a fly in need of a swatter.

Your dependency is really an excessive neediness to the point that he can never completely satisfy you. No matter how close partners are, they occasionally each have to come up for air. Try to give him the impression that you can live without him for the afternoon he needs to take off and go visit his sister for a family conference about his mother. Remember, too, that he has commitments at work and can't always have you by his side, no matter how much he loves you. Let him go to that convention and don't panic as if all he wants to do is get away from you for a day, and that means he is trying to get away from you for a lifetime.

Your dependency is really total helplessness. We are all a little helpless, but yours is a learned helplessness, where the more he does for you, the more you develop a case of disuse atrophy, to the point that you become like a little child who cannot function at all on his own. You can do so little for yourself that you have become less "dependent" than lazy. You have become like Sol, whose cries were, "Dave, get me a glass of water; Dave, can you open the bottle top, it's stuck; Dave, can you figure out how to insert this plug into this socket and anyway I'm afraid to do it because I might get electrocuted; Dave, can you change the light bulb for me, I am afraid it will shatter in my hand and ruin my manicure if I turn it too hard; Dave, can you put my thing in you for me, it's just too much trouble to put it in myself." Men like Sol always act too tired, too busy, or too unknowledgeable to do things around the house, or in the yard, and instead leave everything up to their partner until sooner or later he complains, as happened in one case, in the form of a diary left open by accident for the partner to read, that is, should he get up the energy to pick up the book and turn its pages.

Clearly, if this is you, you have to stop being so dependent and you have to accomplish that feat without simultaneously going to the opposite extreme and becoming too independent. Your goal is to be somewhere between being constantly in his hair and being nowhere to be found. However, if you have to err at all, remember that my research has shown me that partners who complain about their guy's excessive dependency underneath take it as a compliment, whereas partners who complain about their guy's being too independent underneath take it as an insult. So, decide to be dependent, but when you go to it, do it right, and in moderation, so that you make it not something bad for the both of you but a good thing all around.

Now, suppose your partner is more dependent on you than you would like him to be, or than you are on him. Such a partner requires not scorn but special treatment. More than likely he is a very needy man who blossoms with closeness but withers with distancing. If he constantly wants and needs a continuous IV drip of abject admiration, give him something like that. Any distancing on Mel's part frightened Pete because it started him thinking, "Does he still love me, or does he hate me to the point that he is going to leave me?" He felt rejected and started sulking. Then he got mad, had angry outbursts, started fights, and went out cruising just so that he didn't have to any longer endure the frustration and pain of what he imagined to be serious emotional and spiritual neglect. This state of affairs could have been remedied if Mel had just coddled Pete a little, and given him just a bit more support. Even a small thing like telling him, "The house looks great," not, "I hate coming home to this wreck of a place," might have gone a very long way here.

If your partner is in the dependent zone like Pete (and even if he isn't), say loudly and clearly the words all Petes like to hear:

- I love you. (He may know that already but more than likely he will still question it and so will benefit from hearing it over and over again. It reassures him, and helps ease his fears of loss and rejection. Don't only say the words. Also demonstrate what you mean by such actions as touching and rubbing.)
- Our relationship is the most important thing in the world for me.
- I am so glad we are in this together.
- You look great today; you are such a big sexy thing.
- I don't ever want you to go away.
- I want you to have everything that I have. (Does he wear your clothes? Aren't you proud of how good he looks in them? Anyway, why are they "yours," not "ours?")
- So what. (Saying these words when something goes wrong in your relationship is one of the best ways to reduce his fear of being disliked then abandoned over every little thing.)

Here's an example of what *not* to say, even in jest:

You: (noticing an empty spot in the back of his head) You are going bald.

Him: Then you won't love me anymore.

You: (Just kidding) Yup.

219

Here's another.

Him: What a fabulous apartment.

You: I'd buy it if only I were single again.

Always be available to him, no matter what. When he calls never be too busy to talk to him and when he wants you around never be too pre-occupied to go and be with him. Do something as seemingly unimportant as putting him on hold for another call coming in and you just may go to the top of his long list of people who don't treat him right.

Always make certain that he knows exactly what he can count on from you. Many dependent men can adjust to the known devil—it's the element of surprise that they hate. Don't disappear in a snowstorm when he is waiting for you to come home, making him wonder if you have been hurt in an accident. Call to let him know you are safe and exactly when you will be arriving. Chris went out to walk the dogs, then disappeared for two and a half hours leaving a frantic Joe behind wondering where he was. (Chris, himself a very dependent man, did this to get revenge on Joe who had come home late then headed for the hot tub, and ignored Chris for a whole hour.) In many ways a cheap cell phone can do more for your relationship than an expensive commitment ceremony.

All this is a job for a strong, devoted, man, but if you want a permanent partner, and you are up to it, and especially if you are at all even a little dependent yourself (and of course you are; we all are) the rewards are considerable, and right there at the top of a very short list of the good things that can come your way in life.

13

Danger Zone 9: Overcoming Excessive Competitiveness

When gay men go into the competitive danger zone, they love better than they honor or obey. They turn what could be a joint affair into a struggle for power and supremacy. Their lover becomes their rival, their partnership a duel to the death, and the husband who is a success that guy who makes them feel like a failure.

Some competitive gay men, at least for starters, want the man they marry to be young, big, and good-looking. Then, after they get married, they start complaining that he outshines them in big ways, like being more successful than they are professionally, or in small ways, like being the one the dog comes to first or the one whose lap the cat always chooses to sit on. Other competitive gay men, for starters, marry a man they can view as personally, professionally, and physically devalued. While they may grouse that their lover is a wimp and a loser, secretly that is just the way they like him. They want him to be a big nobody because that helps them feel more like a big somebody. Needing to be number one they treat their husband both figuratively and literally like number two. They put him down in every way they can. They henpeck him or encourage him to drink too much, overeat, or neglect his health hoping that he will become the weak and defective guy of their dreams, and if he attempts to rise up they knock him back down, over and over again, hoping that he will finally give up and stay put in his lowly position so that they can retain their spot on high.

Because competition seriously wrecks relationships, more than one or two strong yeses to the items in the following checklist should alert you to the possibility that you sometimes enter a competitive zone where you struggle for supremacy with the man you are supposed to love. Take this as a warning to leave that zone before your guy starts resenting you for constantly needing to best him, and decides to walk out on you and look for someone who treats him more like an equal.

- As much as I complain that my husband is weak and ineffective, that's just the way I like him.
- In my marriage I like to be the man on top, the strong macho one who holds all the power.
- I carefully pigeonhole my marital roles into feminine (bad) or masculine (good), attaching gender identities to neutral acts like housework, then refusing to be domestic, having concluded that domesticity is for sissies, not for real men like me.
- Whatever he has or gets detracts from, not reflects positively on, me. When he accomplishes something good, instead of being proud of him for being great and basking in his glow, I feel blinded by his light.
- There is a finite amount of loot in our relationship, so that what he gets I no longer have.
- If he has more than I have, I begin to think that I have nothing at all and never will.
- If something bad accidentally happens to him, I am secretly pleased and delighted. I tell him how sorry I am but I really chortle because down deep I actually like to see him hurting.
- I criticize him because I envy him and want him to feel defective compared to me.
- I do things to make certain that he doesn't become everything that

he can be. I might set him up to fail just so that I can succeed by comparison. I even give him enough rope to hang himself. One day he fell asleep in the sun at the beach, but I didn't wake him up, I just let him doze, secretly relishing how much his sunburn would hurt him the next morning so that I could smugly think, "What an asshole."

- I bully him and start fights to make him crawl, because when he is down there I feel as if I am up here.
- I take over in all outside relationships. I don't let him get a word in edgewise. I never let him finish a story without correcting him, or adding to it so that I can be the one everyone listens to and admires the most.
- I make sure that when people do any sort of business with us they always refer to and deal with "me," not "us."
- I encourage people to make me, not him, the center of their attention. If they don't I get very jealous. I worry less that he is interested in someone else and more that other people are more interested in him than they are in me.
- I set up triangular situations where I try to get other people to take sides with me, and against him.
- I have to have all the bills in my name and my name alone, and my name has to come first on all our joint accounts. He is right to complain that I am trying to make him invisible.
- I am a workaholic just so that I can make more money than he does.
- I am unfaithful to him just so that I can prove that I am still desirable, and more desirable than he is.
- If he tries to come out from under my dominance, I get angry, start fights, and begin looking for someone else who will accept a subsidiary role in our relationship.
- Though I like him one down I still hate the feeling that he isn't good

enough for me, and dream that a handsome prince (like the ones I read about in the Harlot Romances I devour) will carry me off to a castle so that I can get away from that big nobody who offers me nothing more than a trip around the moat.

• But I would not actually want a prince for a husband, because who has ever heard of a throne that seats two?

In the competitive zone, Jack secretly gloated and felt better about himself when his lover Mack came home with one horror story about how his boss treated him at work, then another about how his doctor just diagnosed him with a serious illness. Every time his guy tried to crawl out from beneath the rock he consigned him to, Jack kicked him back there so that he would stay put in his assigned lowly position. When Mack continued to protest, Jack intensified the struggle to put Mack down, and when that didn't work Jack completely lost interest in his marriage and headed for divorce court so that he could try again to find someone else to play the loser to his winner.

Getting out of the competitive danger zone involves realizing that you win if he wins. Be sure to save the Schadenfreude for yesterday's tired movie star and one-hit rock star wonder and instead enjoy his triumphs, if only by proxy. Realize that the more successful he is, the more you shine in his light; you're not darkened by his shadow. His accomplishments are yours too, both vicariously and by osmosis. If you want to be selfish about it, congratulate yourself for his being yours, and boy look at what you got.

If he is the one in the competitive zone, let him win from time to time. Let there be certain occasions where you simply make up your mind to stay in his shadow for the good of your relationship, and just enjoy the cool of the shade. Stop struggling to be the bigger fish in your small pond, and start, whenever you can and within the bounds of reason, fading into the scenery. Let the spotlight shine on him without hysterically concluding that you have been seriously, permanently, tragically, and fatally upstaged. Meantime, say to yourself "When it comes to my relationship, winning those marital power-struggles-to-the death can make me top dog, but in a pathetically small pound."

14

Third Parties from Hell

Friends and family hold a great deal of power over you and your partner's relationship. They are frequently in a position to either aid your marriage or abet your divorce. So be very careful to protect your marriage from any damage that they might do to it. Yes, when it comes to friends, do everything you can do to have an extended family of straights, lesbians, and gays who care for you as a couple, who provide you with a safe welcoming environment that makes you feel comfortable, happy, and loved, and who will be there for you in times of need. But at the same time root out any friends, whether straight or gay, who try to destroy your marriage. Stay out of the clutches of such people. There is a reason I call them "schwesters from hell."

Schwesters from hell are spousal saboteurs, cut from the same tube as diet saboteurs who for reasons of their own dangle treats before your eyes hoping to keep you from losing weight. Schwesters from hell typically encourage you to wander, and for any number of the wrong reasons. They might: want to keep a cruising buddy; envy you what you have and secretly hate you for having more than they do and want you to have it no longer; be opportunists who see your lover as a potential conquest conveniently fallen into their laps—someone they can make a pass at or a date with without having to go online and typing in their password or their mother's maiden name; anticipate that after the divorce they encourage you to get, you will once again be free and available to be caught on the rebound; be themselves recent divorcees who want company in their misery; have a bone to pick with your lover and want to make sure he gets his by losing you; be simply sadists who enjoy inflicting pain; be Cassandra queens who told you it wouldn't work and want to demonstrate the accuracy of their prophecy, or Nostradamus queens who want to show off the power of their crystal ball; or be sheep in a society where the herd accepts the premise that monogamy is for sissies, and too uncool and stifling for real men, at least for the gay dudes they admire, and want everyone else to become exactly like.

With these things in mind, they bad-mouth your lover in the hopes that you will like him less. They invite you over by yourself to big parties that turn out to be just for you and them, or they ask both of you over for dinner in their remote country home then, when the last train has left, try to get you into bed. They encourage you to join them in drinking and in smoking the bad stuff, or wax ecstatic about the new bathhouse in town and insist that you join them there for a cool experience in the hot tub. Commonly they tailor their philosophy (really their propaganda) to fit their goals for you. Along these lines, some of their favorite cries are "Set him free and if he comes back to you, he is yours," "You will have him more if you try to possess him less," and "A little something on the side only enhances the main course."

Never, never, open the gates for these people, and if they are already inside immunize yourself to what they have to say in order to keep their negative ideas from disturbing your marital bliss. Don't let the bad vibes they send and the bad advice they offer get through to you. Especially don't ever let them harness and enlarge upon your own negativity to your hubby by using and manipulating the disappointment and anger that is always there beneath the surface in many relationships to provoke you to get the divorce they think you might unconsciously be already considering, and only needing a little push to go through with. Certainly, don't start the process going by unloading your troubles with hubby onto them trying to get them to side with you against him. Don't confuse them into thinking that what is just a temporary annoyance with him means that you are permanently displeased with your marriage. Tell them, right out, and in no uncertain terms, that you plan to stay married forever, and ask them to stop trying to break the two of you up. And if that doesn't work, go find a whole new set of close loving permanent best friends—each and every one someone who encourages you to build on what you have, not tear down what you got.

It's helpful to make a list of all the people you know whom you have, or plan to, let into your lives. Pigeonhole them according to the roles they might be playing in your marriage. Make a three column list with the following headings: 1. for; 2. neutral (those who sensibly refuse to take sides one way or the other); and 3. against. Now, play with #1, watch out for #2, and eliminate #3 completely from your life, as they're likely to cause rifts between you and your guy.

Marshall was an old lover of Rich's who wanted Rich back after Rich married Joe. So when all three were together, Marshall might treat Joe as if he were invisible. He would just ignore Joe as if he weren't there. He would speak to Rich but not to Joe, his way to send Joe the message that he wanted him out of the picture. Or he might try to fix Joe up with other people. For example, over and over again he graciously offered to introduce Joe to all the young waiters at a restaurant Marshall was managing. He made a joke out of that, but he really meant it, however much he served that particular tidbit up in jest.

Of course marriage sabotage, like many of the issues I bring up throughout, is not strictly a gay phenomenon. Straight friends can be as troublesome as gay ones. Jane, the mother of a gay man Michael and I both know, kept trying to get me into bed. She must have been into doctors. I reminded her that I was gay, so she offered to put it where I liked it. I reminded her that I was married, so she reassured me that that was okay because so was she.

However, the dilemma is that if you dump all your difficult friends, you may not have anyone to fall back on if your relationship sours. On the other hand, if you don't dump all of your difficult friends (and do so ruthlessly) you might not have any relationship to fall back on when your friendships sour. As a friend I was dumped out of a new marriage many times. It was painful for me, but I understood that as a single man I was a potential threat to the health of the new relationship. So, my advice to you is to think twice before complaining that your husband is keeping you from your friends, and to remember that what you may have to fear the most is the other way around.

Of course, be careful not to antagonize your really good friends. Your new relationship has upset their old balances. Just as introducing your family and friends into your new relationship is going to change your own relationship, introducing your new husband into your circle of family and friends is going to change their lives, sometimes quite dramatically, and not always, if ever, entirely for the better.

When it comes to your in-laws, keep the peace at all costs. Do everything you can do to get along with them, and hope that they will do the same for you. Before you knock them, remember that while they are your in-laws they are his parents. No matter how much he says he hates his parents, at bottom he loves them too. And if he says that he hates them he probably means not basically but reactively, not forever but for today because he feels that they did something unloving to him yesterday. Besides, his family is your family too, so that when you fight with them you aren't gaining a lover, you are losing a mother and a father. They may be difficult people, but like many other difficult people, they can potentially be brought around to become less harsh and imposing. With a little work you just might get even the most problematic in-laws to accept you and your relationship and be on the side of your marriage, not on the side of your divorce.

Here is some practical advice I learned the hard way. Take any anti-gay stand of theirs not only seriously but also personally. Read it as their way of telling you that there is something about *you* that they don't like. Therefore, don't respond solely by becoming an advocate for the gay cause. Instead, in reply do what you can to improve their image, not only about homosexuality but also about you as one particular homosexual.

Mark didn't get along with Frank's parents for many years, but now they are best friends. They ignored Mark forever, and in the beginning even tried to send Frank off to medical school to get him away from Mark. Once Mark's mother-in-law bought tickets for a Christmas Spectacular for the whole family but not for Mark. Ultimately they accepted Mark enough to invite him over for an occasional dinner, only to hurt his feelings when he got there.

She didn't treat her son Frank much differently or much better either. She gave her daughter everything and her son nothing. She didn't even listen to what Frank had to say long enough to know that his job consisted of working with animals. As Frank once said, I thought wistfully, "My mother called me the other day, and when she was on the phone a dog I was examining yelped. That, I think, is the first time that she knew—if she even knows it now—that I work with pets."

Mark could have avoided her completely, but that would only have hurt Frank. So I told Mark that to have all of your lover's love, you have to love all of your lover's loved ones. Then I suggested that he not avoid his in-laws but instead learn to deal with them, following my rules for coping with and managing those difficult people you just have to get along with: compromise; change for them to get them to change for you; coddle them when they are being uptight; put up with a lot, short of eating everything that they put on your plate; and put a good spin on what they do by focusing on their better qualities and downplaying their worse ones.

So, following these rules, instead of complaining when things were less than pleasant and pushing to avoid his in-laws, Mark overlooked a lot, put what he couldn't overlook into perspective, then did what he could to turn his in-laws from adversaries into cooperative, friendly, loving people. He tried to win them over with his understanding, positivity, and reluctance to seek retribution in kind even when they really hurt him. Whether or not he wanted to go over to see them on the holidays, or any other time of year, he would go even though he got very depressed afterwards, and it took him days or even weeks to recover. He just accepted that they felt rivalrous with him and realized that that didn't really count because it was understandable that they found it hard to forgive the guy who took their precious son away from them and made him gay, however unrealistic their take on things may be. He never fought with them, but instead swallowed his pride and hurt feelings and got over his sensitivities almost no matter what they did to him, and he was as nice to them as he could possibly be, if only to avoid putting his lover in a "them-or-me, choose," position, making his lover distance himself from his parents in order to be close to his husband. Ultimately he achieved his goal: to stop potentially vicious cycles of strike and counterstrike from escalating until all concerned became enemies.

Dealing with your own family requires a somewhat different approach. On the one hand try to stay close to them, but on the other hand don't let them make trouble for your relationship by refusing to accept your guy and your status as a married gay man.

I have just about no blood family at all. I miss not having one, and I wish that I could have gotten along better with the ones I had when they were still alive. So, my advice to you is to do everything you can to keep everyone happily together. Don't just up and leave them for him. Avoid having fights with them over him, and instead be a diplomat and peace-maker who fosters the relationship with them not only for yourself but also for your lover, because things being the way they can be with gay men your lover can probably use an extended family besides his own. Stop hurting them by refusing to see anything at all from their point of view. Recognize that, after all, your parents are human too, and probably have as much difficulty in dealing with you as a gay man as you have in deal-ing with them. Very few parents are so bad that you cannot temper your harsh negative feelings about them with a least a degree of compassion for them. Never bitch and complain about them to anyone behind their backs, and especially to people likely to pass on what you say to them. And never, never, never come out to them as a hostile attack. Rather, make your coming out to them simply a fact of life. In other words, help your parents have a gay son. Remember: coming out is difficult, but so is being come out to.

However, do make it a rule that in dealing with your own family you will do your utmost to put your lover first, whenever that is reasonable and possible. Perhaps you can learn from an incident in my life. One day my father stormed into an apartment in New York City where I was liv-ing with my then-husband and told me that I had to move out because I would ruin myself professionally by living with a man. Unfortunately, Daddy wasn't all wrong. Those days if it got out that you were living with a man there would go your reputation in professionally important circles. But Daddy was seriously wrong in at least one respect: he was a "my son the doctor" type of person who didn't take the personal factor into account at all. What about my personal life? Wasn't that important too?

I didn't listen to him, and he didn't convince me to move out. But I had to be strong, and ultimately decide between *his* will and *my* way. I did, however, be sure to let him know that I knew he was coming from his love for me so that even though I wasn't taking his advice it wasn't a rejection of him.

Take special care to not let your family seriously come between him and you the way Brett did when he made a bad choice between his lover Manuel and his mother, Sue. Manuel had a 103-degree fever from the flu. His mother had her fiftieth birthday on day one of Manuel's illness. Brett took off to visit her anyway, leaving Manuel alone and feeling as if he were going to die with no one at his side. That took some fence-mending to recover from.

Be especially careful here if you have a rejection-prone lover, for example one who sees any pulling away on your part as something that reminds him of rejections from the past. If that's the case do everything you can do to reassure him that he comes first. If your family doesn't accept him (like the family who is nice enough until he talks about being a member of the family when they begin to look uncomfortable, as if to say, "You? Our family?") tell them in no uncertain terms that that won't wash. But don't leave it at that. Also offer them suggestions as to what they can do to make amends and improvements.

Involving anyone's family, his or yours, in your fights and arguments isn't likely to serve you well as a couple. Never bad-mouth your lover to your, or his, family in an attempt to try to get them to take sides with you against him. Role play for a moment and imagine how badly he would feel if the negative things you said got back, and they certainly will. As a matter of fact, don't say anything at all, even nice positive things, because it's easy to distort even positive remarks. As far as you are concerned, your relationship is too perfectly low-maintenance to even warrant any mention at all.

It's dangerous to ask his or your family for advice on how to resolve any relationship problems that you might be having. They cannot possibly know the whole truth because you can't or won't tell the whole story; they will say anything to shut you up so that they don't have to listen to two queers having a hissy; and you are giving them a too-good-to-miss opportunity to take your lover's side just to make trouble with your relationship so that they can get you back. Things won't work out much better even if they surprise you and actually take your side, for now it's you plus one or two against him, and that's not fair play. Besides, as third parties you are putting them in harm's way by involving them in your personal struggles. The following scenario is common. You get them on your side, then get back in good with your lover and drop the third party because they did, after all, join you in a vicious attack on the man you love.

15

Handling Breakups

Marriage doesn't always have to be forever. Not all relationships are destined to be eternal. In the beginning all of us are inexperienced at marriage and so may not get it exactly right the first, or even the first few, times around. So, if you are really having serious problems with a lover, don't go into denial where you refuse to accept that there is something wrong with your relationship. If you are constantly unhappy, and with reason, or if you are doing 100 percent of all the giving, accommodating, and submitting, and not getting much in the way of thanks or payback for your efforts and good actions, first try personal enlightenment using self-help methods, and if necessary take a trip to the therapist for individual or couple therapy. But if these things don't work, consider the possibility that leaving him is your best option, and may be the only one that offers you an out of your difficult situation. Certainly don't stay in a bad marriage just because:

You feel overly guilty. Guilt can lead you to blame yourself for everything that went wrong in your relationship even though your partner is at least 50 percent responsible for your marital problems. Guilt can create a self-image problem that leads you to believe that you don't deserve any better than a bad marriage, and make it too easy for you to be nice to and forgiving of him and too hard for you to be nice to and forgiving of yourself. It can also make you excessively empathic and altruistic, leading you to put too good a spin on everything bad that he does and too bad a spin on everything good that you do, and to being overly self-sacrificial because that is the only way you feel upright and moral. It can also lead to your needing to suffer and to your feeling like a failure at everything you do to the point that you just have to turn your marriage around so that at least now you can succeed at something. Also it can make you feel so ashamed of yourself for not being able to work out your relationship problems that you willingly stay in a bad situation just to feel less humiliated for being such a failure.

You accept the premise that horrible marriages are a given for gay men, the equivalent of everyone's feet hurting, so that a bad marriage is your fate and better than no marriage at all.

You are dimly, and with reason, aware that you have actually failed him in some ways and instead of just putting that behind you, you hang around begging for mercy, forgiveness, and just one more chance to do better the next time around.

You have positive feelings mixed in with the negative so that you stay or go back for more abuse simply because you still love him in spite of yourself, and regardless of all common sense. It's hard not to love some abusers. They can be quite adorable in between episodes of being abusive, and even convince you that their abuse of you is itself an act of love, a kind of love pat to the max, for, as they like to remind you, "We all hurt the ones we love the most."

You are stalking him to get revenge for what you feel he did to you, not caring at all that that involves you in an endless cycle of abuse, recrimination, guilt, more abuse, and all the emotional and physical damage that goes along with that, crippling you by tying you down to where you are now and by keeping you from forming a new, healthier, and more enjoyable relationship in the future.

If you do decide to go (and, while others can help you make up your mind what to do, only you can make the final decision about what is right for you), at least think before you act. What's the rush to break up? Impatience and impulsivity can be your greatest enemy. Don't want out one day, peace of mind and closure the next day, and a new hubby on day three. Before you flee, remember to look up at the trees to see if lovers are growing in them. Remember, too, that looking for someone better is at best an uncertain process, and at worst a long and painful one. It's usually so much easier to get a divorce than a new life.

Certainly don't go before taking all the possible consequences of leaving—financial, personal, emotional, and physical—into account. Consider what it is going to be like after you do leave. Carefully anticipate what kind of existence you will have as a single man. Are you a shy, remote type who won't have much of a social life without your more outgoing partner? Do you have friends and family to sustain you and tide you over during the difficult period of adjustment that can take place after a divorce? Saul gave up all his friends when he got involved with Bill. He did this partly to concentrate on his relationship with Bill, partly because he didn't think his friends were refined enough to belong in his marriage (thinking of his marriage as a temple and his husband as some sort of God was part of the problem in the first place), and partly because his dear schwesters made passes at his new lover and tried to spirit him off for themselves. Unfortunately, when he left after three years of marriage he was truly alone—and had to spend the next three years remaking his life starting at ground zero.

If you do go, go the right way. Make certain to do what you can to avoid hurting his feelings unnecessarily. Never walk out on him without warning, or tell him, "So get out," in a fit of pique. I say that not only because you might change your mind and want to apologize afterwards only to have him refuse to take you back, but also because if when you go you treat him harshly he will almost certainly never forgive you, and he may, like many ex-lovers, find little or big ways of seeking revenge. During college I had a lover in the class ahead of me, who, naturally, graduated a year before I did. We broke up the summer after he graduated, partly because he refused to continue to see me, using family obligations as his excuse. The breakup wasn't a pleasant one, and he even smashed the watch I gave him against a wall, after which I refused to speak to him ever again.

Unfortunately, he threatened to get revenge against me by cleaning out all the joint accounts and keeping all our joint possessions. Worse, he came back to college when I was still there in my last year and tried to turn everyone against me, first by saying that we were lovers, which had the anticipated effect because in those days being gay wasn't accepted at all, and second, to ice the cake, by saying that I left him without reason or notice, causing him to have a nervous breakdown which (he lied) was so severe that he had to admit himself to a mental hospital.

Hopefully if you do go you will be in peace afterwards. But some gay men just cannot handle breakups very well. They discover a painful truth—that when it comes to the end of a gay relationship the gay relationship never seems to end. They discover that it is just not true that when there is a will there is a wake. Being gay doesn't protect gay men from having a prolonged grief reaction. Everyone advises them to "just get over it," as if they can because it's a gay thing to move on without looking back, but they cannot. Instead of getting a move on and looking for someone new, they stall and keep going back for more of the same. All they want is him and all they can think about is how to get him to love them again. Meant-to-be-helpful advice like "don't call; don't go back when he asks you to return; and keep a bad picture of him by your phone so that you can remember him in the worst possible light" flows as freely as it falls flat. Strong feelings are at stake here, and the stronger they are, the less they are subject to conscious control. If this is you, what you need is fewer people *telling* you to get over it, and more people *helping* you to do just that.

Start the healing process with **step one** which involves just accepting that you don't have to push to feel better today and get over your grief tomorrow. Don't try to rush things, because you can't. Grief takes time to resolve. Recovery has to go at its own rate and how fast it goes depends on a number of factors, and there are too many of them to be able to predict exactly how long it will take.

It will, however, almost certainly take longer if you are overly pessimistic about your future, thinking that you will never find another man. You just might find one when you are ready, for if you found (and kept) one once that means you are lover material, and lover material tends to seek and return to its own, former, level. Certainly don't feel that just because you are lonely now you will be lonely forever. That's what Mike felt when, alone the first New Year's Eve after his breakup, he panicked and had unsafe sex so many times that he is still amazed that to this day he did not pick up anything worse than hepatitis. He had convinced himself that New Year's Eve represented some sort of deadline for him, and if he didn't make it out of the doldrums by then, he would never make it out at all. This was an artificial, self-imposed deadline, and you shouldn't create one of your own like that.

Step two involves understanding why you are floundering helplessly the way you are. What you need is not a pep talk but real answers to tough questions. Why can't you get over him? What is keeping you stuck in a relationship that you know isn't viable? Why do you still call and keep his picture by your bed, holding on to him in the false belief that there is hope that things will once again be as they were before? Mostly I have found that there is one big answer to all these questions: you can't overcome your anger with him. So often it is anger that keeps a bad relationship alive. The binds of intense anger can be even stronger than the binds of love. Anger makes you feel guilty, and guilt is superglue. You hate yourself for what you actually did (or just thought you did) to him, so you beat yourself up by constantly going back trying to be a nicer, better, person this time around. Instead, burn the self-blame bridge behind you as soon as you possibly can. Don't dwell on beating him or yourself up for what happened to your relationship. Realize that some things don't work out, that we don't always understand why, and counter regrets with the mantra "He just isn't worth it."

If you feel that you are really stuck in a black hole, consider getting into therapy and staying with it until you feel comfortable with yourself once again. The therapist's training and theoretical orientation is important, but more important than that is the nature of his or her relationship to you. Do you feel positively about your therapist? Does he or she seem to feel positively about you? Is he or she there for you in a crisis? Especially if you had an abusive, critical lover, you need an affirmative therapist to undo the hurt. Once I was having marital problems and therapist problems at the same time. All three were against me: my lover, my therapist, and my superego. My lover blamed me for everything, I blamed myself for everything, and my therapist joined in the fray by telling me that I was entirely responsible for what was going wrong in my marriage.

He meant that to be the good news—because if you are responsible for everything going wrong in your marriage that means that you have the fate of your marriage in your hands, and that means that you can make things right. But I was too depressed at the time to hear that part of it, and instead I only heard more of the same critical abuse I was swallowing everywhere and every time I tried to get fed a little love. Even though the therapist was making me worse by being completely unaffirmative to me, instead of finding another therapist I was buying that *I* was the one who had completely screwed things up and would continue to do so unless we worked to radically change my personality and with it my personal contribution to my impending demise. It would have been much easier for me to deal with my problematic relationship if I hadn't bought into the disconcerting negativity that I was hearing all around me, and paying for to boot.

How soon should you allow yourself to fall in love again, and when is it too soon so that you are falling in love "on the rebound?" If you find someone really terrific tomorrow should you go for it today? Should you get lucky don't necessarily assume that you are picking a lover on the rebound. Certainly the mythology is firmly on that side. But don't jump to the conclusion that your judgment is necessarily shot just because your relationship has recently ended. True, it takes time to get over an old lover; and right after a breakup your judgment *can* be bad. But it doesn't have to be. And there are counterbalances to the bad judgment that can occur at such times. Neediness bordering on desperation can be a positive motivator. There is nothing like it to make you less vulnerable to fearing commitment, and nothing like it to help you see the positive side of a new guy who might not be absolutely perfect for you (no one is, anyway). So it's a wash. Besides, life may bring you Mr. Right the day you broke up with Mr. Wrong, and it wouldn't make much sense to throw him to the wolverines just because you think that there is something amiss about the timing. Sometimes a quick new love affair and remarriage is not a rebound phenomenon, it's just a stroke of good fortune. Go for it, but just be extra cautious considering how you might not be seeing things completely clearly at this particular time of your life.

Of course, there is nothing that says you cannot change your mind and go back to the man you just broke up with. How well going back works out depends on what you do when you get there. What should you do with old resentments? Either break up and stay broken up or go back and forget all about them. Going back and dredging them up over and over serves no purpose at all. It's a mistake to go back as the same person then use your lover as an old punching bag repeating all the old problems you had with him before. If you do go back, use the breakup as a wake-up call and as a growth opportunity so that you can become an even more wonderful presence in your man's life, to the point that he can love you even more after the breakup than he did before everything went black.

16

A Difficult Relationship Rescued

I present the case of Ted and Arnie to give you a glimpse inside my treatment rooms so that you can get an idea of the kind of process that is available to you if your marriage is so in trouble that you need the intervention of a professional.

Ted was Arnie's third husband, and Arnie was Ted's second, with each having contributed something big to the demise of their earlier relationship. Arnie's last partner was an emotionally unstable and abusive guy who had a history of just storming out on husband after husband and never coming back. But Arnie, then as now, was no innocent victim either, because he did his share of provoking his guy. Like the time he and his last partner were giving a big party in their country home and Arnie was supposed to bring the food down from the city, but he got stuck in a snow storm, which looked like an unavoidable tragedy, unless you take into account that the forecaster had predicted the storm a week earlier and Arnie could have avoided the whole thing by leaving way before it started.

Ted's last partner was a very critical person, who would complain about Ted both to his face and to their mutual friends. Ted on his part gave his last husband plenty to complain about. For example, Ted complained that his husband, a nonsmoker, didn't want him to smoke in the house. Come to find out, the husband didn't really mind his smoking in the house. What he didn't like was Ted going upstairs to the bedroom and lying in bed smoking one cigarette after another, smelling up the room, soaking butts in half-filled glasses of water, and running the risk of care-lessly starting a mattress fire.

So it's no surprise that even though the day they got married Ted And Arnie seemed ideally suited for each other, they had been together for only a few months when big trouble started.

Arnie's bite was sometimes worse than his bark. His extreme openness and directness, which he alone thought of as "being honest," often hurt Ted's feelings, and a lot. His insensitivity showed early on, in the follow-ing manner. Ted, who worked at home, would clean all day just so that when Arnie returned from work he would tell him, "The house looks great." Arnie knew what Ted wanted, but instead of giving it to him, and offering a compliment, he would come out with a criticism as he first walked through the front door, something like, "I hate coming home to a place that isn't as neat as I want it to be." Not surprisingly, Ted overre-acted, then moped for days complaining that Arnie didn't love him because if he did he would go easier on him.

Arnie could have been much more supportive of Ted in a general way. Instead of "we are all human and no one is perfect" it was "have one accident and that makes you a superklutz." For example, once Ted broke a glass when he was doing the dishes, and Arnie, instead of saying some-thing like "We all have accidents," told Ted that he was all thumbs and reminded him, more than once, that now they only had seven glasses, exactly one short of a complete set, and that this wasn't open stock either, so don't even bother trying to replace the one that's gone.

On his part, Ted could be extremely passive-aggressive to Arnie, so soon it was Arnie's turn to feel the heat. For example, Arnie was washing the dishes when the soap loosened his wedding ring and down the drain it went. Ted didn't scream, and Ted didn't complain. Ted just moped. When Arnie asked him what was wrong, Ted said, "nothing." Arnie asked him again and once again Ted said, "Nothing." Then a month later it all came tumbling out: "After all, it was our wedding ring, a symbol of our love, something that can never be replaced. Yes, you can get a thousand of them at Tiffany's, but it will never again be the same one on your finger, and that's what counts."

Things began to go downhill from there, as criticisms flew and recriminations flew back. Their whole conversation seemed to degenerate into "You did that to me, and upset me," followed by "You *made* me do it; if it weren't for you then…" For example, Ted had a fender bender. Arnie let him have it with "We can't afford your stupid accidents." Ted's reply? Not "I'm sorry, I'll make it up to you somehow," but, "You made me do it; if it weren't for your keeping me up at night I would have been more alert and I would have seen that other car coming."

Soon enough their friends got involved. Emails flew and were intercepted. Kind schwesters reported back what was being said they should know about but probably hadn't heard. A few offered their houses as a place for comic and other kinds of relief, and more than one suggested that they knew a nice boy they could introduce….

It's no surprise that soon their sex life began to suffer. It went from only every few weeks to no one could come no matter how hard they tried, to Viagra wasn't doing it (isn't there anything stronger?), to discussions about having outside affairettes, and even bringing the outside in with threesomes. Not surprisingly, soon enough all eyes began to wander, and pretty obviously. When one complained to the other that he was constantly cruising, the other snapped back that naturally he was because "Anyone married to a loser like you would do exactly the same thing."

Trust and respect became a thing of the past, and anger began to seep out all over. We began to hear words like, "incompatible," "big mistake," and, referring to their late husbands and the demise of their last marriages,

"Here we go again." Arnie once even said he considered going straight. At least he told Ted that not only could he have married someone better, he was thinking of doing it right and getting married properly—this time, to a woman.

Their friends suggested a divorce. "It's no problem," one said, "You are both young and there's plenty of time to find someone else," or "You are both gay and it's a gay thing to move on, so go before you kill each other." "Look at you two," said one particularly unhelpful mutual friend (known to his intimates as the Puccini anti-heroine "Madama Tarantula"), "This one's face is always red from anger, and that one's face is always white from panic. Can't you two be more civil to each other? If you can't stop it, and stop it right now, just get it over with. I know a good divorce lawyer who will help you take care of the paper work and divide the assets. And that marvelous Ted can always come live with me, just in case he has no other place to go."

Fortunately, another, much more helpful, friend suggested couples' therapy instead, and the two of them came to see me.

Instead of getting mad, even, and away, Ted had elected to stay for now. He told me he was staying but he was miserable for all he could think of was "Does he still love me or does he hate me and is he going to leave me?" He sulked, had angry outbursts, and once even sought revenge by cheating on Arnie not with someone who was sexy because he was good-looking but with someone who was sexy because he was a nice guy. Arnie on his part said he didn't care anymore because he was beyond caring, but it was clear to me that he was very hurt that Ted was not only being difficult but was blaming Arnie for everything as well. Both agreed: their relationship was in tatters.

I was worried that the two men were at each other's throats to the point that they needed an emergency big time out to stop the vicious cycling that was destroying their relationship, to say nothing of both of them. I decided that the most effective approach would be to help *Ted* handle *Arnie*. Taking care to avoid being judgmental by shifting all the blame onto Ted, I started by working on ways Ted could better manage Arnie. My goal was to get the healing process going whatever that took, and in my estimate that goal was best and most immediately served by working not with Arnie, though he was the partner who was at least equally troubled, but with Ted, who at least seemed to be, for the moment, the most tractable and the most reasonable, as well as the least disturbed, of the two. As such I believed that it was Ted who was in the best position to do the most immediate good for this troubled relationship. I was in effect using an approach I discovered worked when our cat clawed our dog for trying to play with her. The cat, not the dog, was the bitch, but that didn't matter. We trained the dog because it was the dog that was the nicer, and the more responsive, of the two.

Here is what I said to Ted. "Look, Ted, if you want to rescue this marriage you need to give 90 percent in the beginning. Arnie is a hot potato but not so hot that he can't ever cool down—if you give him a chance and don't drop him first. He is a difficult guy but there are some great things about him and it might be worth it for you to give your relationship your all for, say, six months, to see if you can bring things around. Now here is what you can try to do to defang this particular monster."

I asked Ted to view Arnie as a superheated cup of coffee right out of the microwave—not to be either shaken or stirred, that is, not to be provoked in any way. Sure, Ted was justified in his bitching, but that didn't help matters, because it only had the effect of putting Arnie on the defensive, inspiring him as it did to come up with even more attacks on Ted both to protect himself and to get a measure of revenge.

I asked Ted to try to comfort Arnie whenever Arnie felt troubled. For example, when Arnie came home late from work late I asked Ted to restrain himself from complaining that Arnie kept him waiting and to instead offer him sympathy in the form of understanding. Ted should understand how Arnie must feel having to do extra work without extra pay, having to postpone that evening cocktail, and, adding to his burden, having to worry about how Ted would react if he didn't show up on time.

I also asked Ted to take as much responsibility as he could for Arnie's pissiness. If Arnie came home after Ted had been around the house all day and complained about how closed-in the house seemed, Ted should just admit that the house was stuffy and that he, Ted, having been home all day, had simply gotten used to it, and instead of asking Arnie to stop criticizing him, just offer to open the windows. In effect, I asked Ted to treat Arnie as an enemy nation, keeping in mind that lasting abuse-free marriages are little more than diplomatic triumphs in one's own small part of the world.

I next suggested that should Arnie become abusive, Ted should give him not a hard time but absolution. I explained my reasoning as follows: abusers often feel guilty and self-critical after they come out of their abusement park. It's tempting to think "Gotcha, you bastard," and wring your abuser dry for being evil, but in the long run it can be a better idea to tell him that you survived and that he didn't hurt you as much as he might fear he did. You can say, "I would prefer things to be otherwise, but I have come to accept that that is just the way you are, and I have decided to continue to love you in spite of it." Doing that took a lot out of Ted now, but it promised to make the problem less for him in the long run.

I also advised Ted to try positive reinforcement with Arnie. I suggested that he compliment Arnie when he did something right, instead of just complaining and criticizing him when he did something wrong. For example, Ted would tell Arnie he hated it when he didn't shave. Instead I suggested that each time he did shave Ted should say, "You look so good that way, so sexy."

I told Ted that he needed to set limits on Arnie, but to be sure to set them gently. Sometimes he just had to say "no," but when he did say no he should say it without being final about it, always leaving open the possibility that a "yes" was still in the offing if new information should still come in or if Arnie should change his behavior for the better. He also had to set limits respectfully, saying, "Please, can we?" and, "What do you think?" and afterwards, "Thank you, and I appreciate your doing that for me." He also needed to use an *educational* not a *confrontational* or controlling approach where, instead of ordering Arnie around, he would share his thoughts with him so that Arnie would always know exactly what was expected of him—teaching Arnie what he needed to know instead of criticizing him for what he hadn't yet learned.

In short, I advised Ted to act as if Arnie were going through a bad phase in his life and that the best thing Ted could possibly do was to help him get through it, and the best way to do that was to coddle Arnie, that is, to treat him gently, doing everything he could do to cut him some slack and to avoid provoking him in any way, and continuing in that mode until Arnie felt comfortable and safe enough to start emerging from his difficult hurtful zones.

As Arnie became calmer, I began shifting more and more of the focus to him and his problems. After giving the situation, and Arnie, a few weeks to settle down, I asked Arnie to make a list of all the wonderful things about Ted, then a companion list of all of Ted's problems. Then I asked Arnie to compare the two lists and see whether the good outweighed the bad. I suggested that he might even show Ted the lists, and ask Ted to help him out by not doing the negative things that Arnie said were bothering him.

The negative things Arnie had listed were all little things—things that didn't mean much but that still, right or wrong, drove him wild. Here was the list. *You always leave the bathroom a mess, put wet towels on the bed, forget or refuse to make the bed, spew cracker crumbs all over the place, and don't clean up after yourself when cooking. After I cook a complex meal you insult it by inviting people over "for a simple dinner." You annoy me by first asking me a question then after I answer it asking someone else in the vicinity the same question, as if to say, "He is smarter than you." You are also complaining to others about me and it is getting back.*

I also asked Arnie to stop interpreting everything Ted did in a negative light. That led to a discovery of something that Arnie had until now kept well-hidden—that he was actually jealous of Ted. One day when Ted was watching television and looking intently at the screen, Arnie assumed that he was in fact looking at the male lead's crotch when he was really just looking at his outfit. When Ted came home one day his shirt was in the back seat of the car. Arnie saw that and assumed he had taken it off after a love fest, when the reality was that he had spilled coffee on it and the only way he could get dry was to strip down to his T-shirt.

Essentially I was playing the role of a peacemaker, asking each man to lay off and start treating the other with the respect and kindness due the person they had supposedly chosen as a lifetime partner. My focus throughout was to find ways to maintain the relationship by assigning not responsibility for starting the bleed but things to do to staunch the flow of blood. I had started with Ted. Though he was the one who was hurting a bit more, he was also the one who was in better control of things and more likely to change. My goal was not to point a finger at Ted as if to say he was the one to blame, but to call a halt to silliness from whatever source it came and turn the partners from adversaries into allies by whatever means were available. Most helpful were Ted's comforting words, and a few mea culpas even when he wasn't the one who had opened up or salted the wounds in the first place.

It took six months or so for the healing process to begin in earnest and another six months for it to take hold, but these guys are still married today, twenty years later, and thankful that they didn't give up too quickly and walk out on each other. When I last spoke to them, as they looked back they agreed that if they had given up too soon, they would have prematurely abandoned what in the long run turned out to be a really great committed relationship of a lifetime.

17
Models of a Great Relationship

Jed and Bryan didn't relax just because they were married now. Instead they viewed their marriage as a work in progress—a sacred blessing but still something that needed ongoing respect, care, and concern, as if its very life depended on it. So they gave their relationship regular checkups, and whenever they found something amiss made the indicated repairs as promptly and efficiently as possible.

They refused to view divorce as an option. Right from the start they made the decision to put breaking up completely out of their minds, settle down once and for all, and stick with the man that they had, and for the rest of their lives. They always remembered to keep their wedding vows in mind, and that "I do" didn't mean "I might, let me think about it." Yes, they heard that many people say that 50 percent of marriages fail, but they refused to foresee a bad outcome for their own marriage based solely on pretty shaky statistics. Besides, they realized that pessimism is as much a prediction of the future as it is an evaluation of the past, that bad outcomes are the fruition of low expectations, and that unconsidered refuges like divorce court are the ones least likely sought.

They always treated their man with honesty and respect, the way you might treat a good friend you wanted to trust and love you always. Even when it came to small things, before they did something, anything, at all definitive, they first checked to see what their actions might mean for their relationship. They always consulted with one another to avoid making unilateral decisions. If one was tempted to overspend on gewgaws, he weighed what that would do for his figurine collection against what that might do against his relationship. Even when it came to accepting or declining a simple dinner invitation they thought not, is the food going to be good or is the company going to be sophisticated, but will that favorably input into, or suck some life out of, the two of us. Bryan hated music, so Jed was tempted to buy himself a single season's subscription to the opera. But he didn't, because it would have meant disappearing every Saturday afternoon to attend a performance alone, leaving Bryan behind, probably bored and possibly furious, to the point that his judgment could be seriously compromised, and who knows what he would do next?

Of course, like any other married couple, they did have some relationship problems. They tried to resolve these selectively, letting many be and just trying to work around them using a Zen-like philosophy consisting of "Who cares, "So what," "It doesn't matter in the infinite scheme of things," "It is what it is," "Whatever," "Life happens," and "You did the best you could and what you had to do." For example, though they never could seem to agree on the perfect guest menu, they stifled any temptation to make it an issue of "You never listen to me" and instead decided "They will eat what we serve and if they don't like it there's always the Golden Arches down the block." Whenever something seemed especially important to the one the other would accommodate to him. Once they had a little decorating tiff. They had recently moved, and Bryan wanted a certain cabinet in the bathroom, but Jed didn't think that it looked good at all in there. Jed complained, but Bryan asked "Can you possibly leave it there? I like it." So Jed reminded himself, "After all, so what; who, besides him, am I trying to impress?"

They never actually had a fight. Each time one was tempted to lash out at the other, they instead staunched spurts of annoyance with the tourniquet of empathy and altruism. As far as they were concerned, it didn't make sense that when people get mad on the road we call it "road rage," but when people get mad at home we call it "married life." They always remembered that the president of a large corporation once said that it's usually a great idea to check your tongue and your temper. So whenever they got angry, a little voice inside their heads reminded them to "lay off, because fighting only leads to guilt, misery, and recrimination."

Careful to get their priorities straight, they put their guy first, before anything else in their lives. He went to the top of the list before their possessions, before all strangers including their boss, their coworkers, and (unfortunately, this does not always go without saying) the neighbor they waved hello to each morning, and, whenever possible, before their family. Carefully avoiding treating their dinner companions better than they treated their marital partners, they instead treated each other like customers who were always right, applying the same rules of courtesy and politeness to each other as they applied to their outside personal and professional relationships. They made their marriage-guide books, in addition to the usual ones, books of etiquette written by all the usual writers: Benjamin Franklin's almanac; Aesop's fables; and the Bible. Applying the rules of etiquette and diplomacy to life at home they said "Please" and "Thank you," remembered that flattery gets you everywhere (or as I once put it, "spoiling your child spares his rod"), never hurt the one they loved the most or bit the hand that fed them, kept in mind that the expression "a thing worth doing is worth doing right" applied as much to hubbies as to hobbies, bought into Aesop's implied advice to grab and hold onto the grape you got, and, applying the golden rule to their marriage, remembered that you get back in spades what you shell out in hearts.

They studiously avoided playing the blame or "who did what to whom" game. The one who messed up would take at least partial responsibility for what had happened. For example, if Jed ate too many cookies he blamed himself for allowing himself to be tempted as much as he blamed Bryan for tempting him by leaving the cookie jar out where he could find it.

Of course, from time to time they lost their tempers, but when they did they would apologize afterwards. For example, one day Jed accidentally let the cat out then yelled at her for being an escape artist, then got yelled at by Bryan for stupidly putting her life in danger (first by letting her out and second by scaring her, running the risk that she would panic and keep going). After the incident was over, Jed apologized, saying how much better it would have been if instead of yelling at the cat he had tried a more gentle "Here, pussy pussy" approach, seducing her back in instead of scaring her off. Then Bryan apologized to Jed, saying how much better it would have been if instead of yelling at Jed he had simply pointed out the advantages of gentle persuasion over the disadvantages of scaring the cat by screaming at her. As things turned out, the cat did come back in, Jed said, "You are absolutely right" and "How dumb I was" and "I won't pull that again," and Bryan promised to be more helpful and supportive the next time something like that, or any other accident, happened.

My very successful, very wonderful relationship is based on forbearance, focus, flexibility, perspective, and sacrifice, all of which provide a good portion of the glue that has kept me and Michael together for over twenty years in a low-, or really in a zero-, maintenance relationship, one that is modeled more after Lake Placid than after the Bermuda Triangle. Here's how things work with us:

Instead of fighting we resolve our problems before they snowball. If we disagree about something we recognize that there are two sides to everything, and if we fight at all it is about which one of us will willingly and gladly accommodate to the other. I don't like that show but you do, so I'll watch it with you and see what you like about it; that doesn't belong there but that's where you want it, so that is where we'll put it and I bet it will look better than I think; and I promise not to complain about construction delays on our new apartment until May 31 if you promise me that if work doesn't start by then we might start looking for someplace else. Also when one of us goes astray, which is mainly me, the other forgives because we know that if you forgive your partner *today*, he will be so appreciative that you will likely have less to have to forgive *him* for *tomorrow*.

Perhaps the most fortunate thing of all is that Michael knows exactly how to handle me. He just disregards my temporary lapses into zonal insanity because he knows that I will soon get front row and centered again, and if I behave badly he gives me more than one chance to do better. That endears him to me to the point that I actually have fewer lapses in the first place. For example, long before we even got married, one day Michael stuck a note for me on the door of my house with adhesive tape. When I pulled the note off the paint came with it, making me furious with Michael. Michael ignored my anger and didn't let it affect our relationship. I regretted my actions ever since and learned not to behave that way again, a principle that I wouldn't have been able to put into practice if Michael didn't give me a second chance.

Correction: I did it again when Michael invited his whole family over for the fourth of July without first asking me if it were okay. I went on and on complaining, and in a public place too. To this day I don't know what came over me, but Michael just stood there and didn't say a word until I got out of that zone. Because he didn't respond or challenge me, the tirade became mine alone. If he had responded negatively in kind my tantrum would have turned into our fight and I would have no doubt forgotten who started it and felt first provoked then second justified in lashing out, instead of feeling that I was (as I was) wholly responsible and stupid for starting the whole thing up in the first place.

Also Michael never criticizes me when I do dumb things. For example, today I left the butter out of the refrigerator. A whole stick of butter was ruined and had to be thrown away. Other people would have gotten very angry with me for being so wasteful. But Michael just laughed, remembered that as a struggling writer I make back in a year what I ruin in butter sticks in a day, and just tossed the butter.

The end result of his forbearance is that I don't walk around with my head between my legs, feeling sheepish all the time and angry with him for making me feel like a stupid fool. Instead, feeling good enough about myself to want my life and our relationship to go well, I feel strong enough to be able to do what I have to do to make it stay that way, and motivated enough to want to calm myself down to avoid destroying what I already have.

From my end of things, I love him so much and so want my relationship to work that I gave up drinking completely, knowing that alcohol made me temperamental. I also stayed completely away from mood-altering substances knowing that they caused me to lose control of my anger. I learned that a mind un-stoned and un-drugged is a mind in control of its emotions, in the head of a person in control of his behavior.

Of course Michael isn't perfect. Sometimes he has annoying and even potentially dangerous habits. He occasionally leaves the metal squeegee he uses to swipe down the shower door on the soap dish, so that it predictably falls when I get in and slam the shower door closed, even hitting and gashing my foot. What do I do? Scream that Freud would have said that he has a secret death wish directed to me? Or just ask him to leave the thing elsewhere and to make sure I remember to check to see if it is poised to drop before I get into the shower.

Sometimes he gets as sticky as I do about minor things. Michael likes to buy magazines from the rack, while I like to get magazine subscriptions.

Michael's point is that while it costs more that way, it isn't as much fun, and besides the magazine people constantly bombard you with all kinds of annoying promotional advertising to get you to renew. We are both right and both wrong about this, but I smartly pull back instead of stupidly digging in. Generally speaking when there is any difference of opinion at all, whenever possible I let Michael prevail, because that is more important than my dominating him and having my way. I know that all differences of opinion are just clashes between two truths, with one truth rarely significantly truer than the other, and I learned long ago that a successful marriage is all about each partner realizing that there's a reason why they make both chocolate and vanilla. So our marriage thrives because we both learned over the past decade that while all our troubles are small change, all the joy of our relationship is big bucks.

About the Author

Photo by Jim Saylor

Martin Kantor, MD, is a psychiatrist who has been in full-time private practice in Boston and New York and on the staffs of the Massachusetts General Hospital and The Mount Sinai School of Medicine. He is the author of thirteen other books on psychological topics, including a revised version of *Distancing*, which describes how people avoid relationships due to anxiety; *Paranoia*, which covers such disorders of the paranoid spectrum as paranoid personality disorder; *Homophobia*, which views homophobia as a manifestation of deep psychological problems; and *Treating Emotional Disorder in Gay Men,* which describes the form some common psychological difficulties take when they appear in homosexuals and offers some practical suggestions on how to modify psychotherapy to make it more relevant to, and palatable and affirmative for, gay men. *My Guy*, which offers single gay men some practical suggestions on how to meet the Mr. Right of their dreams, was published by Sourcebooks in 2002. His most recent work is an article on coping among victims of sexual prejudice and discrimination for a book on the psychology of prejudice and discrimination. He lives very quietly during the week with Michael, his partner of twenty-two years, in an apartment in Asbury Park, New Jersey, and reverse-commutes to New York City on weekends.